Nail Scarred Hands Made New

Nail Scarred Hands Made New

Making Sense of the Gospel
in a Violent Latin American Slum

JOHN SHORACK

WIPF & STOCK · Eugene, Oregon

NAIL SCARRED HANDS MADE NEW
Making Sense of the Gospel in a Violent Latin American Slum

Copyright © 2012 John Shorack. All rights reserved. Except for brief quotations in critical publications or reviews, no part of this book may be reproduced in any manner without prior written permission from the publisher. Write: Permissions, Wipf and Stock Publishers, 199 W. 8th Ave., Suite 3, Eugene, OR 97401.

Wipf & Stock
An Imprint of Wipf and Stock Publishers
199 W. 8th Ave., Suite 3
Eugene, OR 97401
www.wipfandstock.com

ISBN 13: 978-1-61097-838-5
Manufactured in the U.S.A.

All scripture quotations, unless otherwise indicated, are taken from the Holy Bible, New International Version®, NIV®. Copyright ©1973, 1978, 1984 by Biblica, Inc.™ Used by permission of Zondervan. All rights reserved worldwide.

William Carey Library Publishers for use of the following chart: The Secular-Animistic Axis from Gailyn Van Rheehen's book *Communicating Christ in Animistic Contexts*, page 96.

Though many have fallen in the streets of Caracas, the death of Caligallo took on unusual significance for our small team of mission workers in the city's slums. God used this tragic moment to usher us into a new season of faith and hope, of life and vision for God's shalom—even in the midst of pain and suffering. For this reason and more I dedicate this book to his living memory, which *will be told wherever* I announce the Good News.

Contents

Foreword ix
Acknowledgments xi
Introduction xiii

Part 1: Partners at the Cliff's Edge

1. Brother Caligallo 3
2. Family Dynamics 11
3. The Running and Pleading Father 21
4. Which Jesus? 28
5. My Enemy's Savior 37
6. At the Cliff's Edge 47

Part 2: Partners at Cornelius' House

7. Spiritual Power Encountered 53
8. Spiritual Power Reassessed 65
9. God's Spirit Crosses Lines 74
10. God's Spirit Incarnates 83
11. God's Spirit Works Paradoxically 92

Part 3: Partners outside the Gate

12. What Is a Kid to Do? 99
13. What Are the Faithful to Do? 106
14. What Did the Faithful One Do? 113

15 What Did the Apostle Do? 115

16 Biblical Hope Revisited 119

17 Partners in New Creation 129

Afterword 139
Appendix: Some Thoughts on Teaching a Nail Scarred Hands Made New Gospel 142
Bibliography 147

Foreword

OUR NEIGHBORHOODS ARE DEAR to us. Across five continents, InnerCHANGE team members have forged relationships of such intimacy with neighbors, and together celebrated personal moments so dear, that it has felt like we were experiencing ministry more than "doing" it. So we have been cautious in discussing the sober reality of violent crime. Furthermore, we have seen that those who have never experienced life in our landscapes can too easily misconstrue the issue of violence in slums, barrios, and inner cities around the world as *the* issue confronting missionaries.

    John Shorack's book, *Nail Scarred Hands Made New*, is searing in its honesty about the danger of violence and the impact of loss in pursuing solidarity with Christ among the poor. But it is also a book that is lavish in its hope and insightful in the way it identifies Christ's redemption steering along the jagged edge. John writes that in order to thrive on tough mission terrain, one must move beyond the category of "mission worker" to embrace a deeper relationship as mission partner with Christ, whether at the edge of the cliff of offense described in Luke 4 or at the edge of the manger of vulnerability in Luke 2. In a book that combines tender memoir, scriptural meditation, and theological reflection, John stakes out new ground for people who are earnestly seeking to pursue Jesus to the margins. It is not simply what is being said here in this book that is powerful. It is what is being lived.

    I am fortunate in that some of my very closest friends are colaborers in InnerCHANGE. We are an order among the poor that is part mission, part tribe, part family. I have known John Shorack for more than twenty years and have had the privilege of mentoring him as a leader in much of his first decade serving with us. We have always been open, honest, and very tight. So when he first began to sense the Lord leading him and his family to Caracas, I struggled a bit. I was concerned not simply because a move to Caracas meant a move away from regular physical contact but also because our explorations in the hillside slums above that capital city revealed that we would have to anticipate a level of violent crime we had not encountered before. I was especially concerned because John lost his father to the Vietnam War when he was a boy, and the impact of that loss was incalculable for John and his family.

So the possibility that John could walk in his father's footsteps and be taken from his wife and three children at a tender age was all too real. Did I talk about this with John? I can no longer remember. But spoken or unspoken, the possibility that John could die in Venezuela and leave his three children fatherless was understood. John has been threatened violently and robbed many times in Caracas, yet he has continued to show great trust and fortitude. And yet, as he makes clear in this book, he and his family have thrived and glimpsed a depth of security and intimacy in Christ that could perhaps have been gained in no other way.

It has been more than twenty-six years since I moved to a unique place called Minnie Street in Santa Ana, California, and founded InnerCHANGE. Within a few months of relocating there, I realized I was on sacred ground that called for a New Testament Jesus. There was both so much need and so much opportunity for the gospel. And yet, Minnie Street was so far removed from the reach of the church.

One afternoon while I was sitting at my front window listening to the sounds of hundreds of children down in the courtyard, I was conscious of my inexperience in the face of such need. More important, I was conscious of my inadequacy in the face of such a privilege; that I should be allowed to minister in such a place simply overawed me. In that moment, I prayed earnestly in my simple apartment that God would bring better people than me to that street, better people than me to InnerCHANGE. God has answered that prayer time and again since that afternoon. *Nail Scarred Hands* is evidence of the fruit of that prayer.

John Hayes
General director of InnerCHANGE

Acknowledgments

A WISE FRIEND WITH published works to his name kindly educated me one day when I rather proudly put before him my "final draft." Not unlike a sensitive father who praises his five-year old's first colorful stick drawing, he tenderly explained to me that there are "three kinds of drafts . . . one that's for yourself, another that's for an audience, and finally, one you write for a publisher." He let me connect the dots. I swallowed my pride and admitted to myself that I had not come as far as I had thought.

Many have helped bring my fledgling manuscript to the point of publishing. In the earliest, most painstaking stage (when I truly didn't know which end was up), my brother Todd gave way too much of his valuable time. I think he's forgiven me for what I put his editorial skills through. Later, my uncle Lloyd Johnson took the time to coach me in my self-editing skills. Thank you! In the home stretch, my InnerCHANGE colleague and friend, Catherine Rundle, provided big-picture editorial instincts that the project needed. Her enthusiasm for the book also spurred me on at a critical juncture.

Two individuals inspired this journey of reflective writing. Bob Ekblad, whose visit to our team in Venezuela played a central role in what gave birth to this project, represents so much of what is needed in the church today: courageous leaders who build bridges long enough to reach across the widest divides in the body of Christ. Vishal Mangalwadi penned a little-known book in the 1980s called *Truth and Social Reform*. Tucked away in the last chapter is a beautiful treatise on hope from his context of poverty in India. His insights into Christian hope, chiseled out of his experience of persecution and hardship, took the blinders off my eyes for a rereading of biblical passages that helped me connect the dots between suffering and hope, between our part and God's. Without Vishal I don't know if I would have had the courage to address the whole matter of suffering.

Many others have encouraged me along the way. InnerCHANGE colleagues and friends John Hayes, Mark Smith, and Darren Prince have cheered me on, believing in me at each stage of the manuscript. The Caracas InnerCHANGE team has exercised great patience with this never-ending project that inevitably pulled me away from team commitments. My wife, Birgit, has been a constant source of strength and encouragement along the slow and often arduous path it took to get to the final line (thank you!).

When I reach back further, I remember with great fondness a day while studying at Fuller Seminary, when a visiting speaker named Tom Sine came to give a talk. At the conclusion of his speech, his challenge to seek first the kingdom of God struck a chord with my buddies and me. Carl Johnson, John Macy, Grant Power, and I, were meeting regularly with a mentor named Viv Grigg, who had come to campus to inspire students to give their lives in the slums. At that moment, through the word spoken in the meeting and in the faces of my friends on the journey, I knew—we all knew—this was the life for us. And here I am today. ¡*Mil gracias!*

Introduction

ANOTHER DAY, ANOTHER MORNING bus ride in the big city. Caracas, a city of at least seven hills and six million tightly packed inhabitants, lies at the foot of a beautiful mountain range that stretches the length of the city's narrow, ten-mile corridor. First impressions are everything here, and as a first-time visitor entering the urban core from the airport, you cannot miss Caracas' slums. From every inch of freeway to every crowded street corner, they are ever-present, always visible, spotting the city's many hillsides with their makeshift red-brick dwellings.

This is the city that's been my home since 2001. I live with my family and a small mission team on one of those hillsides in one of those red-brick homes.

Caracas, Venezuela

On this particular morning, I managed to ignore the pulsating beat from the bus driver's stereo enough to read the morning paper while simultaneously noticing two young men that boarded the bus. They made their way to the back of the unusually empty twenty-four-seater, sitting directly behind me, just inches away. Without taking my nose out of the paper or even diverting my eyes, I noted to myself that these were possible *malandros*—Venezuelan street criminals. On the heels of that thought came another: they could put a gun to my neck if they wanted to. I read on, my mind consumed with national and world events.

Five minutes later I was shaken out of the news by the realization that the bus was being held up! The two young men had gone forward presumably to pay and get off. One of them pulled out a handgun, which he pointed at the driver. His accomplice made his way to each passenger, taking jewelry, cash, and cell phones. There were only six or seven passengers, including myself.

The young man took earrings from the woman directly in front of me and the other to my right, both seated within inches of me. Not wanting problems, I made a special effort to demonstrate my compliance. I began taking out my pocket money. For reasons God only knows, the young men never acknowledged my presence. I tried to get their attention, assuming I was next in line. Inexplicably, I was invisible to them. They moved to the front of the bus and jumped off. Nothing short of an act of God spared my wedding ring.

I would not be so fortunate the next time. Within a few weeks two young men on another bus noticed my ring, threatened me, and stole it. Then three young men jumped me in yet another incident on a bustling commercial street in downtown Caracas. While shopping for school clothes with my two daughters, one of them threatened to shoot me while his buddies reached into my pockets and took everything I had. Marna, my nine-year-old daughter, screamed to attract attention, hoping someone might come to my rescue.

I became traumatized as a result of these experiences. I found myself consumed with the notion of dying. My mind wandered to my childhood and the loss of my father. My mind turned to my own children—Johanna (13), Marna (10), and John Mark (9). "Lord," I prayed with tears welling up, "I don't want to die yet! I don't want to leave them without their dad."

My perception of reality became distorted. How dangerous is life in Caracas? I lived fifteen years in a dangerous inner-city neighborhood of Los Angeles, California. The sound of gunshots was routine for my family. I coined an adage that helped me explain the danger to the occasional visitors who ventured into the neighborhood to see us: "Anything can happen at any time, though most things won't happen most of the time." In that city we witnessed the violence without being targeted ourselves. Gangsters considered us off-limits. In Caracas, no such social buffer exists. They target Venezuelans and foreigners alike.

Taking greater precautions, I continued walking the hillside, visiting homes and riding public transportation. But to make matters worse, a teammate and I were held up at gun point fifty yards from my home during a routine walk at dusk. I felt confused and insecure.

My mind replayed the stories of all the people I had met since visiting Caracas the first time in 1998. The first words I learned after stepping off the plane at Simon Bolivar International Airport were *malandro* (a delinquent youth who commits street crimes and kills people) and *inseguridad* (lack of safety). On that trip I encountered many people gripped by fear of street crime. Now, several years later, I honestly cannot think of a Venezuelan with whom I have shared my story who has not responded with a similar, if not more dramatic, experience of their own.

"T.O.A.": TRAUMATIZED ON ARRIVAL

Two months after getting jumped in downtown Caracas, I boarded a plane for the United States to attend meetings of the InnerCHANGE leadership team. I remember my arrival. It was a Friday evening. From the moment I touched down I wanted to talk. I needed to talk.

I talked first to the friend who picked me up at the airport, then to the twenty guests who had gathered at his home to welcome me. The next day I met one-on-one with several people. In seemingly endless conversations, I dwelled on the crime and violence in Venezuela. I was consumed with the notion of dying. Try as I may, I couldn't change the topic.

Sunday morning I went to church in the Mid-Wilshire district of Los Angeles. The turn-of-the-century gothic structure contains a traditional sanctuary replete with stained glass windows, oak pews, crimson-colored carpet, and pew cushions.

The service concluded and I hung around to greet people. When the sanctuary emptied, I passed through the large doors to the foyer. As I did, I greeted an elderly usher. At that moment, while my hand was in his, I remembered a jarring story my brother Todd told me.

Todd, two years my senior, had visited Geneva, New York, the upstate college town where our family lived in the 1960s. He stood up in the First Baptist Church during Sunday morning worship and introduced himself as a visitor: "My name is Theodore J. Shorack III." The small, aging congregation gasped in disbelief. Thirty-three years earlier they had sent off a promising young father of four named Theodore James Shorack Jr. to fight in a distant war. When he didn't come home, they inscribed his name in a stained glass window as a memorial to my father.

That sanctuary was also large and traditional, with permanent, hardwood pews and crimson-colored carpets. After the service, my brother also mingled with church members until the sanctuary was nearly empty. And when he passed through the heavy doors into the foyer, he too met an elderly usher. As they shook hands, the man told him, "I've been an usher in this church since the sixties. I knew your dad well. I'll never forget his last Sunday before leaving for Vietnam. I shook his hand on this very spot and I heard a little voice, like a whisper in my ear: 'He's not coming back.'"

There I stood, shaking the hand of an elderly usher at an old church in Los Angeles, California. In my trauma, the story of my dad's death flashed through my mind and shook me. *I'm due to return here on furlough next year. Does this mean I will die in Venezuela before then?* I wondered to myself. Was this a word from God? From Satan? A product of my fears? I felt confused and troubled.

Depressed and defeated, I pulled my suitcase and troubled spirit to Fifth and Olive Street to await a city bus. This was back when downtown Los Angeles became a desolate place on a Sunday afternoon. Buildings and streets lay abandoned, the quietness out of character. A haunting wind whipped up the paper trash, giving it the eeriness of a ghost town. City buses passed every sixty minutes, if that. I took my place at the bus stop with some folks that looked worse off than me.

When I got to Pasadena, I pulled my suitcase to the campus of Fuller Theological Seminary, where I studied missiology nearly two decades earlier. I had an hour before my friend was to pick me up. I sat down, pulled out my journal, and found company with my heart. So much was going on inside. As I put my emotional churning on paper, tears flowed. I didn't want to die. I thought of my children.

My journal entry from that day:

> I feel closer to death. It's weird and kind of morbid. Part of me resists putting words to these thoughts, yet I can't deny the feelings that are so close to the surface that they pop out in conversations that inevitably touch on my life in Venezuela and my fulfillment of a dream there. Satisfaction and death . . . they go together—like Simeon, I feel a depth of satisfaction in Venezuela that enables me to say for the first time: I'm ready to go. I've seen my dream. I've touched it.

A strange thing happened. Even though I see in retrospect that my emotions played games with me and that my perception of reality became twisted, God used this drama to do a new work in me. I came to terms with what I was feeling about the price we're paying to live in Venezuela with all its risks. Was I ready to die? Was I willing to die in Venezuela? There, in the commons area of the campus, sitting alone with God and my turbulent heart, I found a place of rest. Somewhere in my tears I came to a moment of release, when I could joyfully and tearfully declare from deep within my being, "Yes, Lord. I can go." In that moment, the sun broke through the clouds that covered my soul.

My friend arrived. I was ready—to die, yes. But also to live.

I am a mission worker with InnerCHANGE, a Christian mission community whose vocation is to live and work with the poor as a sign of God's kingdom. My wife, Birgit, is from Germany. We met in Southern California and together started the InnerCHANGE team in downtown Los Angeles where our three children were born: Johanna (1990), Marna (1993), and John Mark (1995).

As mission practitioners in poor communities around the world, we place a high premium on context. We rarely, if ever, open a new work with a pre-made plan. We let the place and its people speak and inform us. We take time to grow in the host culture, listening and learning our way into a slum community. For these reasons, this book is very contextual, with reflections that have tangibly risen out of the streets we walk, the worldview of the people we love, and the history of the place where our children call home.

This could sound rather romantic. It's not. To live and work in a violent slum is to look evil in the face in ways I was never prepared for by my comfortable upbringing in middle-class America. This challenge gets exasperated by the generally pessimistic outlook we inherit regarding the world-at-large. Irreversible climate change, insurmountable conflicts in the Middle East, recurring famine in Africa, and the hypocrisy and arrogance of politics that exploits and dominates in the name of "freedom" and "democracy" are but a few of the woes that besiege us with hopelessness. In my childhood these remained largely abstract. Moving into a slum community put flesh and blood on many of these destructive powers. Without a solid grounding in Christian hope, I couldn't survive, much less thrive, over the long run.

To thrive long term we must also be more than workers. My use of the term "partners" in the section titles is not inconsequential. Because InnerCHANGE mission workers cultivate a three-pronged identity of missionary, prophet, and contemplative, the partnering with Jesus that I envision ("at the cliff's edge," "with Cornelius," "outside the gate") reflects a prophetic stance *and* a spiritual union. We don't simply do the radical thing. We do justice *with* Jesus. Or, to use Pauline terms, *in* Christ and "in step with the Spirit." This is something I explore in the coming pages.

One of InnerCHANGE's most pronounced values is what we refer to as "the upside-down kingdom." For us this means that God's ways are radically different from ours and that much of what the world—and the Church—esteems stands in polar opposition to what God esteems. In our literature, we state it this way:

> We will minister low to high, that is, from the bottom rungs of a society upward, remembering that significant aspects of God's kingdom are often lodged in the humblest crevices.
>
> We will not despise faithfulness to small things in favor of the big picture, believing that the kingdom of God is upside down with regard to many of the world's values.

In many ways my reflections develop this motif from fresh angles. I do this by employing a narrative theology model that holds together three intertwining threads: (1) urban slum realities, (2) the biblical text, and (3) the practical expressions of the church in mission. This method uses a contextual story as the launching point for missional reflection.[1]

Several theological influences merit special attention because they provide the paradigms that shape my reflections: Kenneth Bailey, Tom Wright, Vernard Eller, and Justo González. Though not represented by an author per se, the ministry of the Toronto Airport Christian Fellowship and the revival associated with it represents yet another paradigm within which my reflections take place. In the final chapters, authors Vishal Mangalwadi, José Míguez Bonino, and Jacques Ellul provide invaluable insights that bring the loose ends together. Only later in the writing process did I realize the influence of Lesslie Newbigin and the concept he calls "the logic of election."[2]

One comment about the prodigal parable is in order since it figures prominently in the book, and I lean heavily on the insights of New Testament scholar Kenneth Bailey. In the context of Luke 15, Jesus tells three parables in response to the murmuring of the Pharisees and teachers of the law over his fraternizing with "sinners." His intent with the stories is to explain his mission. Throughout *Nail Scarred Hands* I freely associate the younger son of the parable with sinners *and* gentiles. Kenneth Bailey does *not* do this. I do so because I believe it's consistent with Jesus' ministry and message to which the parable testifies. (As a case in point, in Luke 4:25–30, the "younger son" of Jesus' message to the synagogue was Namaan the Syrian and the widow in Zarephath, both gentiles.)

Finally, though I am a lifelong member of InnerCHANGE and ooze so much of what we collectively hold dearly, I don't write in the name of our community. Nor do I intend to represent the views of my colleagues. I do hope that what I have written will inspire those embarking on InnerCHANGE-like work in urban slums of the world.

---

1. Van Engen and Tiersma, *God So Loves the City*, 241–64.
2. Newbigin, *Gospel in a Pluralist Society*, 80–88.

Part 1
Partners at the Cliff's Edge

1

Brother Caligallo

IF IT'S TRUE THAT street crime hits in waves, then Venezuela has been struck by a tsunami-like ocean torrent. Some believe the quake behind this began in earnest with the people's uprising in February 1989, when an IMF-pressured austerity package forced then-President Carlos Andrés Pérez to abruptly and dramatically raise basic commodity prices, including bus fares. In a knee-jerk reaction, thousands from Caracas' hillside slums took to the streets in violent protest. More than one thousand lives were lost in three days of bloody bedlam in the capital city. One researcher coined a shift in the *modus operandi* among streets criminals as a move from "I will rob you" to the more sinister "I will rob and kill you." He believes this change took root at this moment in the country's history.[1]

In spite of efforts from opposition groups to blame President Chavez for the growing murder rate, no one disputes that the problem known as *inseguridad* (lack of safety in the streets) topped the populace's list of most pressing issues prior to Chavez's ascendance to the nation's highest office.

Even in the face of widespread danger and violence, our approach to mission in the turbulent slums has been anything but a big splash. Venezuelans have at various times described our work as that of ants (*hormigas*). We serve unassumingly, without drawing attention to ourselves. We're small in number, a relative drop in the bucket, yet hardworking and united in effort. At first glance little seems to be accomplished. Yet in the end, no one with eyes to see can deny the profound impact of our consistency.

---

1. Moreno, *Y Salimos a Matar*, 52.

My wife and I arrived in Caracas with our three children and two teammates in November 2001, two years after a political tsunami brought the larger-than-life populist Hugo Chavez to the presidency. Our teammates returned to the United States in 2004. They were replaced by two others, and then another. These co-workers also left after a three-year period of service.

Caracas street crime didn't become personal to me in the first year or even the second. When the wave finally hit, it hit hard, as I wrote in the introduction. The two stories that follow come from two teammates that lived through this particularly hot season when the pressing issue of *inseguridad* in the streets began to burn in our hearts. Corrie Long, a recent graduate from Wheaton College, served on our team from 2004–2007. Ryan Mathis, a young man in his early twenties who penned the second story, worked with us from 2006–2008.

John's neighborhood

A LETTER FROM THE SLUMS

Several months ago, I [Corrie] asked you to pray for the surge in violence we were experiencing here. At that time, I was held up by two young street thugs who tried to take the gold ring off my finger. They got the purse off my shoulder, but I put up a fight with the ring and the guy couldn't get it off. The ring itself is inexpensive, but it was a gift from my parents and I've worn it since I was thirteen! I got a bit roughed up and scared, as you can imagine. In my nearly three years in the barrios ("slums" and "barrios" are used interchangeably), this was the first time I got held up. Now I want to tell you about an answer to prayer that came out of the experience.

Several weeks ago I found out that one of the *malandros* in the neighborhood was recovering in a nearby hospital after getting shot. The young man's name was Caligallo—the very guy who tried to steal my ring. Since that time, Caligallo had been terrorizing the neighborhood. The more I heard, the more I learned of his story.

Caligallo grew up in the neighborhood as an orphan. His brothers are in jail or dead. His sister sells herself up the road from me. With nothing to hope for and no life to believe in, Caligallo fell into what surrounded him: the drugs and violence of the streets. Our neighbors watched him grow up, fed him, and even tried to help him along the way. Since choosing this path as an adolescent, they seem to be waiting for him to be killed off. No one has hope for him. "May God forgive him," they say, "because we won't."

News of Caligallo's situation arrived on a Friday afternoon. My friend from the street, Diana, invited us to visit him in the hospital. When we arrived at his bedside, my team leader John, my teammate Ryan, and I (all of whom Caligallo has robbed) just stood there a little awkwardly, and perhaps a little fearfully. Yet soon we were talking, laughing, even holding his hand. We prayed for him and over him—simple prayers, thanking God for his life. We shared smiles and jokes. We told him that our team was praying for God to spare his life and that this was an answer to our prayers. We told him that we cared about him and his life. The forgiveness in the room came *alive,* as if God walked among us. We stood there on holy ground, a living demonstration of Christ's pardon to our wounded offender.

As we parted, he reached out and held my hand, the same hand from which he tried to rip my promise ring. Yet because God is good, there we were again. With a glance I told him that he was forgiven . . . in the deepest sense of the word. When I felt Caligallo holding my hand in such a different way, looking me in the eye and saying, "Gracias, Corrie," I was overcome by the beauty of God's gift.

Corrie

We didn't know if Caligallo would die in that hospital bed or once he hit the streets. Now he is back in the neighborhood, though in hiding. My teammate Ryan has become his friend and seeks him out.

Visiting the sick and loving my enemy—the guy who makes me fear walking to the team office every day—humbles me. Yet this is why I want to be here. Isn't this what Jesus' kingdom is all about, redeeming the awfulness through forgiveness? I'm not saying our visit changed his whole perspective on everything and that his life will be different. I think there was part of

Caligallo that was proud to be lying there like a wounded street soldier. Change comes so hard, if he even wants it.

IN RYAN'S WORDS

A friend and I had the opportunity to minister God's radical love to one of my neighborhood's most infamous outcasts, Caligallo. I felt an impression from God urging my friend Chris and I to bless Caligallo and pray over him. I felt comfortable with this divine nudging because Caligallo and I had been developing a friendship ever since he was hospitalized after a rival street criminal shot him on my street corner. I had already prayed for him a couple of times before our visit that day, and he had always been very receptive. It was obvious that he respected my concern for his life, and I always tried to treat him with dignity.

It was a Thursday when we went to his house. We made small talk for a while, and then I told him that we had come wanting to pray God's blessing over him. I asked him if that was alright. He said, "Of course." Before we prayed over him I told Caligallo that I had a gift for him. I handed him a poster of Jesus' face. I liked this poster because Jesus' eyes are defiant, like he's determined to change things (unlike the more common images of him as a helpless victim). I told him gently, "I know you steal, because that's what life has come to. I know you take things from others. But this is something that I want to give you. It symbolizes all the good gifts that the God who loves you wants to give you without you having to steal them." Then I spoke the words that had been running through my head all week whenever I thought of Caligallo, words that I believe were a message from God for him. "All week I have held the words 'God is *for* you, God is on your side' in my mind and heart. I think they are words for you. Even though I am saying them, I hope you can take them as the words of God himself being spoken over you. 'Caligallo, I am *for* you.'" Then I prayed for him, speaking God's blessing on his life.

Ryan

After this I turned to Chris, who had not said much because of my banter. I asked him if he wanted to pray for my friend. He smiled and sat pensively. Then he looked straight at Caligallo and said, "I'm listening for anything that God might want to say to you right now, because God loves to communicate with his children, and *you* are a child of God." Suddenly Chris asked, "Do you ever hear yelling around your house at night?" (Chris gets mental images and impressions from God.) Caligallo said he did and that it kept him from sleeping. I probed further, asking if he thought the screams sounded like they came from people or spirits. He immediately said, "Spirits or ghosts." Chris explained that Jesus has power and authority over everything in the world. He has even given us, his followers, power to cast out evil spirits. Chris led us in a prayer of rejecting the spirits' authority and casting them out. Then we invited Jesus' reign to be there in that place "on earth as it is in heaven." The beautiful thing was that Caligallo, the notorious street criminal, had his hand outstretched, as both Chris and I did, in the direction of where the screams came from. He was taking an active part in the prayer!

After that, feeling that the place he lived might be full of evil, I asked if I could pray for peace inside his house. He shyly led us into his ramshackle house made of loose pieces of oddly-shaped scrap wood, perched precariously at the edge of a modest cliff. I could see the embarrassment on his face as we entered his bare, one-room shack. At eighteen years of age, he lived alone in what was once the home of his deceased mother. I couldn't hide my surprise at the huge hole in the wall overlooking the precipice, big enough to fit a refrigerator through—not to mention an enemy or two.

We stood there for some time talking and learning more about his life. We continued to speak words of blessing and love to him. Finally we went home. Two days later we heard the news: "Caligallo has been murdered. They stabbed him to death!" Chris, knowing the deep sorrow that filled my whole being, threw his arms around me. I wept for Caligallo, an orphan gone drug addict and criminal. I wept because he had become my friend, and I had known in my chest God's scandalous love for his prodigal son.

The days following his death were filled with the anguish that comes with mourning. I went to his wake and his burial. I held his death like a plague in my bones until I could release my own suffering and grief to God.

Many people in my neighborhood rejoiced at Caligallo's death. He got what he deserved, they said. The people carried out God's justice. If you've committed harsh crimes, you must pay for them with harsh punishment.

Yet is that the whole story? Is this how God sees the story? God is just, to be sure. Nevertheless, his mercy goes beyond his justice so that we can affirm with the apostle Paul, "Where sin abounds, grace abounds even more."

As you can imagine, street violence became a burning issue for the team and me [John]. We didn't have answers. We weren't even sure of the right questions. Yet we knew that something had changed, something inside us, and that God would use this *something* to also work through us in the slums where he had called us.

2

Family Dynamics

WHEN A YOUNG LIFE gets snuffed out in bloody vengeance, life feels fragile and precious, somehow sacred. Emotions hit hard and wide, from anger to sadness and every shade between. The sadness I felt was not only for the loss of Caligallo. I grieved for what I can best describe as veiled hearts and minds. It was as if on the stage of life our vision was blocked by a thick, heavy curtain. Try as I might to look beyond the curtain, I couldn't. My vision was impaired. I, like my vengeful neighbors, didn't see Caligallo the person. If it weren't for Ryan's determination to break the ice socially, my fear would have kept me away from my offender. My belief in the neighbors' condemning judgments of the feared *malandro* would have gone unchallenged. Nor did I see God clearly. After Caligallo was gone, I longed to see the bigger picture of what God was up to.

My prayer became, "Lord, pull back the curtain! Grace me with eyes to see your unfolding drama." The following reflections come from this prayer—to see with unveiled hearts and minds, to see the story behind the story.

My use of the parable of the prodigal son leans heavily on the work of Kenneth Bailey, a New Testament scholar who lived and worked in the Middle East.[1] The parable provides glimpses "beyond the curtain" that reveal God's hopeful story in this season of pain and sorrow. Bailey's unique contribution to biblical scholarship is his cultural knowledge of traditional Middle Eastern peasantry, which has remained remarkably similar from the time of Jesus to the present. The dynamic interfacing of the parable with barrio experiences opens up inspiring and compelling theological vistas.

---

1. Bailey, *Cross and the Prodigal*.

There was a man with two sons. The younger one cursed his father by asking for his portion of the estate. With money in hand, the son went to a faraway land where he squandered his wealth in reckless living. The older son stayed home and worked hard on the land. After a time, the younger son's money ran out. To feed himself, he worked the most disgraceful jobs imaginable. Then he came to his senses: "I don't need to suffer like this. Even if my father makes me a hired hand until I recover the money I wasted, it'll be better than this." And he set out for home.

Meanwhile, the father had been waiting for his son's return, watching each day from his front porch. One day, while the lost son was still far off, his dad saw him and was filled with compassion. He ran and threw his arms around him and kissed him. No one could believe their eyes when the father came running down the road like a bloody fool.

"Father, I have sinned against heaven and against you. I am no longer worthy to be called your son." "I will hear none of it. Quick," he called to the servants, "bring the best robe and put it on him. Put a ring on his finger and sandals on his feet. Bring the fattened calf and kill it. We must celebrate! For this son of mine was dead and is alive again. He was lost and is found." And the party began.

The older son was in the fields. When he came near the house, he heard the music and dancing. A servant informed him, "your brother is back and your father is throwing a party for him." The older son went ballistic and refused to go in. So his father went out and pleaded with him. The son answered, "Look! All these years I've been slaving for you and never disobeyed your orders. Yet you never gave me even a young goat so I could celebrate with my friends. But when this son of yours who has squandered your riches with prostitutes comes home, you kill the fattened calf for him!" "My dear son," the father replied, "you're always with me, and everything I have is yours. But we had to celebrate and be glad, because this brother of yours was dead and is alive again. He was lost and is found." (Luke 15:11–32, my paraphrase)

THE PRODIGAL

Ryan appropriately calls Caligallo a "prodigal." Like the younger brother in Jesus' parable, Caligallo wandered away from home and squandered his life and his God-given inheritance in reckless living.

As important as the younger son is to Jesus' story, and Caligallo to ours, have you ever asked yourself why the parable is named after the prodigal? We all but ignore the older son while marginalizing the father's importance. The story contains three main characters: the father and his two sons. Solid arguments could be made to cast the older son into the protagonist role. Doesn't the suspenseful ending ride on his moment of reckoning to enter the party or not? The father too demands special attention. As head of the family and the one who tries to restore things, he is indisputably the representation of Christ, dramatizing Jesus' mission in simple yet stirring hues.

As we'll discuss later, the evangelical church has obsessed over the prodigal, making him the heart and soul of the parable. This has led to a lopsided, reductionistic vision of the gospel, something we will look at soon enough.

THE OTHER SON IN THE MIRROR

Perhaps less obvious than Caligallo's role in our barrio parable is the similarity between my neighbors' attitude and that of the older brother. Yet my neighbors' judgment against Caligallo finds good company in the prodigal's older brother, who judges him unworthy of the father's acceptance and embrace. The offense I encountered in conversations with neighbors while (self-righteously?) trying to help them see God's mercy and forgiveness for Caligallo is not unlike the offense the father faces in his conversation with the elder son.

Our 'peace' corner where Caligallo died

Before we get too comfortable with likening my neighbors to the obstinate older son, let's be honest. Haven't we all reacted like the hardworking, "deserving" older brother at one time or another? If we're honest about human nature, we're more like him than we wish to admit. Under ordinary circumstances we, no doubt like the elder sibling, manage to conform to the expected norms of moral conduct. Most of the time we control our anger and do what's right.

We can also concede that it isn't every day that our little brother returns under such extraordinary circumstances or that our father displays such extravagant compassion to an undeserving rat. Yet for the older son, his brother's return precipitates an unparalleled crisis that puts the normally well-behaved brother over the edge.

When we lift our eyes beyond the narrow, exclusive preoccupation with the reckless younger son, previously unseen family dynamic come into view.

TWO HEARTBREAKERS

"I've been slaving for you and never disobeyed your orders . . ." From listening to the older son you'd think the father is a taskmaster. The older son has been living with his father, conceivably his whole life, yet doesn't seem to know his father. Rather than resting on first-hand experience of his father's abundant generosity and graciousness, the older son seems oblivious to such qualities and solely preoccupied with his own performance.

What about the older son's claim that he never disobeyed his father's commands? Bailey points out that in traditional Middle Eastern culture, the expected role of the older son would be to intervene and become the mediator between family members in the face of the younger brother's shameful request. Instead, the older son, as vv. 12–13 imply, remains silent and passive, accepting the division of the estate in which he receives his half.[2]

The older brother becomes furious at the news of the party and refuses to join in. When he speaks to his father, he breaks the protocol of respect and honor by launching into a lecture. He never addresses him as father.

Bailey points out here too that it's difficult for us to imagine how insulting his behavior is. He suggests that to better appreciate the nature of the older son's conduct, we should imagine a wealthy man hosting a black-tie, candlelit dinner for prestigious guests, only to have his son show up at the door unshaven, without shirt and shoes, verbally attacking the host. This analogy, according to Bailey, is too mild to convey the revolting nature of the older son's behavior. Whereas the younger son's request for his share of the estate embarrasses his father privately, the older son embarrasses him in front of the whole community.

What sins does the younger brother commit in that faraway land? Certainly he wastes his money on prostitutes and the like. Or does he? The Greek word for "squandered" does not connote immorality. The word means he lacked discipline with his money; he failed to watch his finances. This is important to note.

How do we know that he slept with prostitutes? Curiously, this information comes from the mouth of the older brother. How does he know what his younger brother did? He doesn't. The comment is the

---

2. Ibid., 44–47.

elder brother's attempt to destroy the restored relationship between the father and his younger sibling. In the context of their community, the elder son knows that if he can make the story stick, no father in the community will give his daughter in marriage to his little brother.

The older son did indeed work diligently in the field. He completed the many tasks that he knew were important to his father. But what does he miss? Where does his blindness lie? He can't see himself and the true nature of his actions. He blindly uses his stature and fine reputation as the responsible older child to try to ruin the restored relationship between his father and brother. He is also blind to the true character of his father.

Rather than reading this parable as the story of a lawbreaker (the wandering young man) and a law-keeper (the dutiful older one), we must read it as the story of two heartbreakers, for *both* of them break their father's heart.

LINE DRAWING

"Do not judge, or you too will be judged. For in the same way you judge others, you will be judged" (Matt 7:1–2). Isn't the underlying assumption of Jesus' command that no one is exempt from the snare of sin and guilt? The point isn't the grave sins my neighbor might have committed. It's whether I recognize what I've done. When I truly see myself and my actions for what they are, I dare not judge my neighbor. Jesus honored "sinners" and gentiles, who by outward appearances didn't conform to the standards of decency or that of the Torah-abiding citizenry. Yet unlike the religious insiders, the outsiders saw themselves truthfully and knew they needed God.

One day during this episode Ryan pulled the blinders from my eyes with his provocative query: "Do we really know if Caligallo has killed anyone?" The question alone forced me to question the source of our data and the neighbors' preoccupation with Caligallo's sins. How much of his reputation was earned, and how much of it was fabricated by the "older brothers" of our community?

We will never know the exact truth. According to Jesus, this misses the point. Drawing a sharp line between "us" and "them," the "good guys" and the "bad guys," inevitably multiplies the bad guys' sins. Whatever sins Caligallo committed against the community, we can be certain that the neighbors multiplied them, feeding their justification for revenge.

Some might object: Aren't you judging your neighbors for breaking relationship with a street criminal? I hope not. I'm no different from them. My neighbors were too afraid of Caligallo to talk to him. They didn't believe it possible to have a normal conversation with him, even though many knew him from birth. I too was afraid to approach him.

I also dare not judge my neighbors because I *am* different. As a newcomer to the neighborhood, I don't share their long and beleaguered history of conflicts, misunderstandings, and offenses. The collective accumulation of anger and hurt in the slum escapes me. This clearly gives me and my team greater freedom to develop hopeful relationships.

There are other factors that make it easier for me to be a friend to Caligallo. We are mission workers who are cultural outsiders, and the trajectory that our neighborhood relationships take is *into* the community to identify with the life of the barrio. We take our missional cues from the "word made flesh," who was sent in the humility of human flesh to redeem all flesh. This incarnational gospel propels us into the world "as the Father sent the Son" (John 20:21).

We pursue this missional lifestyle while simultaneously benefitting from additional identities that we never lose—our country of origin, our history and language, our family, and our mission community. These deeply meaningful sources of strength provide us with a wider, diversified sense of home and belonging. More important, they lie beyond the slums and therefore cushion us in incalculable ways.

The felt-need of evangelicals in the barrio is to separate from their neighbors. The slums, and this city, are their only world, their only place of identity. For this reason, the world and its destructive currents pose a much more serious threat to them. If local believers lower their guard by fraternizing too closely with "bad" people, the "worldly" forces that surround them will snatch away their new life in Christ. To intentionally remove social barriers with the world is considered unwise, even foolish. Moreover, their motives would be questioned if they were seen hanging out too much with immoral people.

ABSOLUTIZING

Line drawing between "decent" people and "unworthy" people creates a false either/or, an artificial choice between good and bad. With a wide angle lens, such line drawing falls within the broader human propensity for absolutizing that which God relativizes.[3] To absolutize something is to make it an unchangeable standard, an ultimate reality—something to be adopted, not adapted. When we absolutize a cause, a strategy, or a doctrinal interpretation, we become dogmatic and closed. In our thinking and attitudes we become air tight, unwilling to engage in dialogue with a perceived enemy who could threaten our stance. We cannot love and respect those who hold different views. Though unspoken, the thinking is this: "When I know that I'm right, and that God is on my side, why would I play host to the devil and his schemes?" This attitude precludes any dialogue.

In the political jargon of Washington, DC, this becomes, "We don't negotiate with terrorists." In first-century Palestine, it was, "We know the Christ doesn't come from Galilee" (John 7:41) and, "If he were a real man of God he wouldn't defile himself with sinners" (Luke 15). In some churches you hear, "Everything must be done with decency and in order." In others, "Heaven is our destiny and soul winning is why we're here." In Venezuelan politics, the slogan of the current government is "Fatherland, Socialism, or Death."

What do these statements have in common? They absolutize that which we hold dearest. Even though some of these causes might be worthy of our concern, they become anti-gospel and destructive when we give them an authority that belongs to God alone.

Here lies the beauty of our friendship with Caligallo. God used this young man to teach us that a street criminal is much more than a street criminal. Caligallo was a human being (alas, much like myself!). In the parable of the prodigal, the older brother absolutizes his position and status as the worthy son. He deems his brother unworthy, leaving no room for negotiating the matter. To accept his younger sibling as no different than himself—equally guilty and shameful in his actions, and equally welcomed by their father's embrace—was an unacceptable impossibility.

---

3. Eller, *Christian Anarchy*, 1–47.

OUR NON-ABSOLUTIZING SAVIOR

In Luke 20, when Jesus entered Jerusalem, the teachers of the law sent spies to trap Jesus in his words. The plan they hatched assumed he operated within their framework. Jesus confounded them because he revealed a fundamentally different way of seeing things. The question they posed to him was: Is it right for us to pay taxes to Caesar or not? The question assumed a closed system, a world of absolutized options. Caesar was all-wrong. Israel, with its God-given covenants and law, was all-right. Classic, air-tight thinking. Jesus, they thought, would be forced to reveal his true allegiance. He was either with them or against them. To their surprise, Jesus didn't fall into the trap. Jesus' spirituality was different from theirs. He didn't absolutize the Israelite establishment and its nationalistic cause. Let's look at what he did.

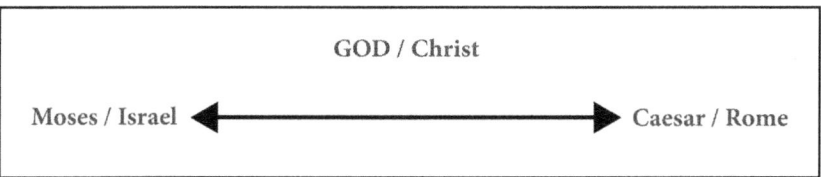

Jesus took a position above the polemic that pit Caesar against Moses. Does this mean Jesus betrayed Moses and the Jewish nation? It means Jesus didn't equate Israel and its interpretations of things with God's. Concretely, it means Jesus wasn't in step with an Israel whose self-perception didn't permit them to accept their pagan neighbors as objects of Yahweh's love and affection.

Am I suggesting Jesus advocated a laissez-faire faith in which ultimate beliefs don't matter? The counterpoint to not absolutizing isn't the lack of strongly held beliefs. Jesus held beliefs just as fervently as the scribes and Pharisees. Where, then, does the difference lie? Jesus' only absolute was his heavenly Father. He didn't believe in Israel the way he believed in his heavenly Father. Nor did he believe in Moses the way he believed in Yahweh, the God of Moses.

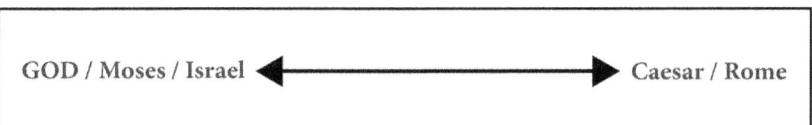

The teachers of the law, chief priests, and Pharisees saw these matters differently. Note that in this diagram their nation is at the extreme left of the horizontal line, with God on their side. To the Jews of Israel, their nation and their understanding of themselves were absolute. To acknowledge that God could be present among a pagan nation like Rome was tantamount to heresy and worthy of condemnation. God was on Israel's side and against their pagan neighbors. Jesus, on the other hand, removed himself from the false dichotomy. He refused to inhabit the either/or continuum where Israel and Rome dwelled at either extreme. By granting primacy to God alone, Jesus relativized his attitude and allegiance toward both. Neither Caesar nor Moses represented ultimate reality. Nor were they to wield unquestioned authority. Both were flawed instruments with limited powers.

To relativize Rome and Israel didn't make them equals. Jesus didn't treat them as if they were one and the same. Rome was Rome, Israel was Israel, and God's purpose for each was unique. In the prodigal parable, the father's heart beats for both sons, even as his love expresses itself differently to each.

Jesus is Savior of the whole world. Though this bald declaration may appear cliché, there's an edge to it that is often lost. God's primacy over all nations translates into Jesus' defiling himself and the Twelve by spending two nights in a Samaritan village (John 4). By seeing God's supremacy as rendering all other causes *relative* to God's ultimate Lordship, Jesus affirmed a Roman centurion's faith as greater than that of "anyone in Israel" (Matt 8:10).

In declaring himself and his mission as the truth (John 14:6), Jesus spoke as one with absolute authority. We, his followers, get tripped up by lending absolute authority to our interpretation of Jesus. As "older brothers" in God's family, we believe we see truly, when in fact we see through a glass dimly. With family dynamics like this, we need a very special father.

3

The Running and Pleading Father

IMAGINE THE FATHER'S SORROW as he looks down the road day after day, waiting for his "son that was dead" to return. Grief over his son's foolish heart keeps him awake and vigilant. Though overcome with joy enough to throw a party when the son comes home, his grief continues. He laments his older son's refusal to join the celebration.

Before Caligallo was killed, I knew his days were numbered. My grieving had already begun. After he was gone, my compassion for Caligallo translated into sorrow for my neighbors. Their exuberance at the news of his elimination stabbed me in the heart.

I can imagine the father's sorrow also peaking, like Ryan's and mine, at the likely comments from the incredulous townspeople. "What on earth's going on?" "I can't believe what I'm seeing!" "How could a father do such a thing?" "What a disgrace!" "What that boy needs is a good spanking!"

The dad in the parable is wealthy, a man of dignity and respect in his village. Imagine the son's entry into town. Typical of that time was an affluent core where the wealthy homes stood. Men of such stature wore robes down to their ankles. They moved gracefully in keeping with their social position. To run to his son, the prodigal's father gathers up his robe, exposing his legs as he runs. This creates a scene that humiliates him before the neighbors. Yet his compassion compels him to gladly suffer public ridicule for his returning son.

Though nothing I experienced compares to the father's humiliating act, I felt foolish and was treated as naive for pursuing friendship with a criminal. After Caligallo's death, Ryan and I made attempts at defending Caligallo as a human being and God's love as being big enough to reach such a "bad guy." Neighbors wrote us off as out of touch with the real world. In a small way we shared in Caligallo's humiliation.

Corrie's joy in the hospital, though nothing like the father's, was still remarkable. She exuded a gladness that welled up in her as praise and thanksgiving for a lost child of God who received her forgiving presence. As Corrie honestly reported, this joy came only after overcoming her fears. True love risks stepping out as the father does, running and embracing first without knowing how such a lavish display of compassion will be received.

We can imagine the villagers knowing of the son's dishonorable departure. The young man's reputation is in the mud. The shame attached to his disgraceful request is unimaginable. Such a step is unheard of and irreparable. His father's careful eye on the road reflects a genuine concern that if his boy reaches the village and is recognized, the people may ridicule if not assault him.

As they stand together in the road, reuniting and restoring that which was broken, the young man no longer fears the hostile townspeople and their rejection. His dad's overwhelming display of approval powerfully disarms the onlookers.

All the younger son hopes for, in his own words, is a measure of compassion from his father: "Treat me like one of your hired hands." Jesus' hearers no doubt resonate with this prospect. They, like many of us, would reason, "Yes, let the boy first acknowledge his guilt and then regain his father's good graces as a hired hand." The villagers will surely want to cut the young man off from community life, believing that the father, at best, might relent enough to allow him to work on his estate. They likely envision the father's response to the approaching son as one of disgust and anger. But that's not what happens.

Remember Corrie's ring? *He held my hand, the same hand from which he tried to rip my promise ring. Yet because God is good, there we were again. With a glance I could tell him that he is forgiven.* Remember Ryan's poster? He gave it to Caligallo with the words, *I know you take things from others. But this is something that I want to give you. It symbolizes all the good gifts that the God who loves you wants to give you without you having to steal them.*

Ryan and Corrie tapped into the beauty of the parable's father. They acted like the forgiving dad, who freely *gives* the wandering heartbreaker what he has *taken*. By asking for his share of the father's estate, the son wishes his dad's death. He takes his dad's life. Remarkably, the father says "yes," giving him what he asks for. Upon the son's return, his dad's hug, not unlike Corrie's extended hand with the promise ring or Ryan's unmerited gift to one who had stolen, boldly declares to the son, "Here! I give you—freely and, yes, costly—more than the inheritance you wrongfully took from me. I give you my love, my trust—my very self!"

With Corrie, Caligallo received more than the ring. He received a hand—a hand extended in forgiveness, love, and trust. With Ryan, Caligallo received genuine forgiveness for wrongs committed and acknowledged: *I know you steal, because that is what life has come to.* The father too knows his son's follies. He doesn't sweep his wayward ways under the rug as if they never happened. He knows that what the son needs is a gift greater than his sin.

CALVARY LOVE REVISITED

How can a father be so happy in forgiving a scoundrel like that? Yet could this be what God in Christ did at Calvary? "God demonstrates his love for us in this: while we were still sinners, Christ died for us" (Rom 5:8). What a foolish God we have! While we were still street thugs, uppity religious snobs, and well-intentioned but misguided crusading believers—so unworthy of mercy—God surprised us by suffering the humiliation of a Roman cross for us.

If my neighbors are right, this means that God is out of touch with the real world. Does the father wait to see if his youngest child has repented before starting to run? Before taking him in his arms? Before showering him with kisses?

No. The father forgives the younger son *before* the boy confesses his sins. Dad initiates. He opens his arms in an unexpected act of forgiveness and reconciliation. The son simply falls into them. His repentance doesn't open the dad's arms. According to Kenneth Bailey, even this gives the son too much credit.[1]

Bailey believes that, according to the text, the son's reason for going home is to fill his empty stomach, not to reconcile with his father. The phrase that he "came to his senses" is more accurately rendered, "the son returned to himself." In other words, he realizes a way to save himself from his predicament. He crafts a speech to manipulate, not to repent. It

---

1. Bailey, "Four Misconceptions."

resembles Pharaoh's speech to placate Moses to stop the plagues. The son doesn't ask to become a slave; he wants to become a worker so that he can repay his own way. In this condition the son starts his journey back to the father—with dirty rags and a contrived speech.

What a foolish dad! According to my instincts as a father who wants to raise sound children, the father's behavior smacks of poor judgment and irresponsibility. Don't I first confirm that my gestures of reconciliation will be received, that my efforts to make things right will be reciprocated? Contrary to such logic, the father in Jesus' parable believes his love will be enough. His forgiveness will transform.

Scripture supports this view of God's work on Calvary. Hebrews 9:26 states, "He has appeared once for all at the end of the ages to do away with sin by the sacrifice of himself." The reference to sin in this text doesn't highlight my sin and yours so much as the big problem of sin: that of humanity's. God, in Christ, did away with the sin that separates us from God. This brings to mind John the Baptist's declaration upon seeing God's anointed one, "Look, the Lamb of God who takes away the sin of the world" (John 1:29).

GOD'S SHALOM

The father in the story stands with the restored younger son, taking the verbal abuse upon himself, yet *without turning his back on the older son*. There's not a shade of dispassion or neutrality on the father's part. He stands with one while moving toward and calling the other. His loving action toward one never compromises his obvious love for the other.

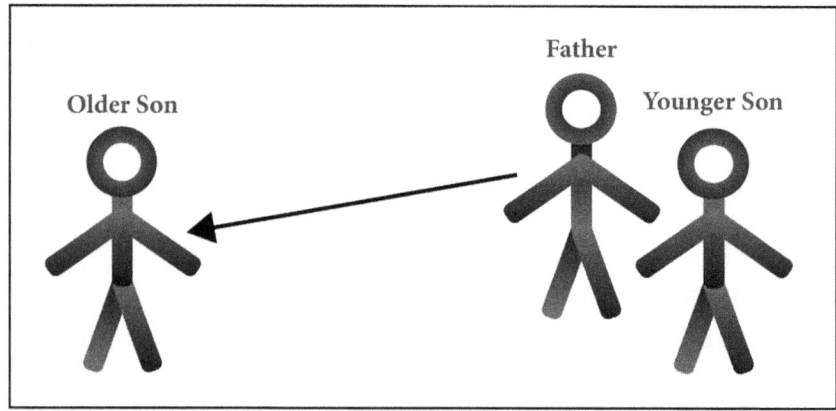

In the father's love for both sons, witnessed first in his running out to the younger one then in his stepping out from the party to plead with the older, we are endowed with a breathtaking glimpse into the vastness of God's nature. With the former, he embraces the one who wills his death for selfish gain. With the latter, he initiates reconciliation with the one who, in self-righteous decency, tries to destroy the restoration of the family by insulting his dad with public ridicule. This provides a beautiful window into God's covenant faithfulness, a snapshot of God's righteous, saving actions that restore us to the shalom for which we were created.

A SMALL SIGN OF GOD'S BIG SHALOM

Caligallo held up my friend José at gunpoint. While his buddy held the gun to José's head, Caligallo took my friend's shoes. A few days later, José told me about the incident. I was struck by the shame he felt walking home barefoot through the web of slum homes where nothing happens covertly. From José I learned how hard it is for a moderately macho man who follows Jesus to consider alternatives to plain and simple revenge.

Let me be clear. We need to reach the Caligallos of the world. Yet we must also reach the "decent" people with the gospel of the pleading father. Without a church that renounces the absolutizing of Christian decency and uprightness over against the unworthiness and badness of the Caligallos, we won't see God's kingdom come or his will done.

Consider this passage from Jesus' most famous sermon (Matt 5:43–48):

> You have heard that it was said, "Love your neighbor and hate your enemy." But I tell you: Love your enemies and pray for those who persecute you, that you may be children of your Father in heaven. He causes his sun to rise on the evil and the good, and sends rain on the righteous and the unrighteous. If you love those who love you, what reward will you get? Are not even the tax collectors doing that? And if you greet only your brothers, what are you doing more than others? Do not even pagans do that? . . . Be perfect, therefore, as your heavenly Father is perfect.

Verses 43 and 48 are clearly linked in Jesus' train of thought. Our heavenly Father's perfection is his divine capacity to love those who oppose him. Yet to pursue reconciliation with my offender in imitation of the Great Lover requires a conversion of the heart.

After Caligallo stole his shoes, I discussed and prayed with José about God's love for Caligallo. Later, I found out that he went to his offender and gave him fruit as a gesture of good will. José also asked for his shoes back. His request was denied.

What enabled José to approach the unapproachable Caligallo with a peace offering instead of a pistol? In conversations with him before his bold act, José was honest about his struggle. He didn't brush over the conflict as if it were nothing. It was extremely difficult for him to view Caligallo with anything other than harsh judgment and condemnation. I don't believe José felt anything close to compassion toward his enemy. He more or less accepted the idea that God could view Caligallo with mercy.

Thin as this foundation felt to him, José was open to new perspectives as we talked through the situation. Contrary to his instincts, and even a bit begrudgingly, he was willing to treat his assailant as a person with a name. To come in peace would require this. Finally, José took a risk that looked foolish to others. By stepping out in unexpected vulnerability, he granted Caligallo the chance to respond in kind with perhaps a surprising word or gesture that could make reconciliation a possibility. What happened in actuality was closer to a truce.

More important lythan the results or lack of them was the faith that José exercised. His modest step represented a movement in the spirit of Jesus' primacy over the absolutizing of good and bad people. As the "older son," he reached out to the "younger son," though hesitantly and cautiously. I can't say that José went into the party. Yet his initial move in that direction can be affirmed as a hopeful sign of God's shalom through the breaking down of dividing walls.

RESISTIBLE SHALOM

This movement—first to the street to receive the wayward younger son, then to the older son who remained outside the party—is powerfully demonstrated by Jesus who "suffered outside the city gate" (Heb 13:12). On the cross, God's act of unexpected vulnerability and surprising forgiveness echoes the heart of the running and pleading father. For God's peace/shalom is incomplete without both expressions of his compassion.

Curiously, the writer of Hebrews takes this next step: "Let us, then, go to him outside the camp, bearing the disgrace he bore" (13:13). This is a hard step for us to take, one we resist. We don't want to follow Jesus "outside the camp" as a "cursed one" or an "unclean one" (Gal 3:13; Lev. 13:45–46). This is when being "in Christ" is the last thing we want.

The dilemma we face as the elder sibling is not only estrangement from our adversary ("this son of yours"). Our rejection is more fundamentally a rejection of God's lordship (the father's authority), evidenced in our refusal to reconcile with those we're at odds with. We don't want to celebrate together as family.

In the parable, the father demonstrates his authority by bearing the shame of the younger son in such a way that blindness is exposed, prejudices revealed, and self-interests laid bare. With the words "this brother of yours," the dad exposes his firstborn's true heart while reasserting his authority to define the relationships. Then, in the heat of the moment with emotions running high, the father's shockingly tender response to the older son's abusive treatment shakes his hearers to the core: "my dear son."

The elder sibling tries to redefine the relationships by taking himself out of the family equation. The father then exercises a loving, mature authority without shaming the son for his insolent behavior. He simply reasserts the true nature of the family.

God's vision of restored humanity requires more than converting the masses that, like the younger son, know they are in trouble and need restoration. What the Bible describes variously as shalom/peace, justice, the new man/humanity, or new creation remains incomplete without restoring the decent, law-abiding, proud ones, too. Nobody gets left out of this kingdom equation.

Yet this doesn't come without a cost. I liken it to a holy clash with the Almighty. In biblical terms, this offense is called a "stumbling block." The father and his two sons embody this divine conflict.

This, of course, leads us to Jesus, the storyteller himself. For he is the one to whom the parable points and whose mission it portrays.

4

Which Jesus?

I TOSSED AND TURNED through the night. Something was troubling me, and I couldn't shake it. Why did I react so strongly to the pastor's advice?

Our small team of North American workers was new to Venezuela, having arrived just months before. The political climate of the country was tense, with the nation divided between government supporters and powerful opposition groups. Our meeting with the pastor was advisory in nature but not political in any way. Yet it must have been obvious to him that we didn't appreciate the gravity of the political instabilities the country was experiencing. It was his parting words that left me so unsettled: "Stick to Jesus," he said. "Whatever you do, stick to him."

What does it mean to "stick to Jesus" in a politicized context where my decision about which morning paper to buy in the open market will be interpreted in terms of my political leanings? As a foreigner, and an American at that, people watch me closely. Even under normal circumstances local people are quick to observe my smallest acts and make their own conclusions.

The pastor's concern was legitimate. As InnerCHANGE missionaries, we live and work in solidarity with the poor. In Latin America, "working with the poor" smacks of Marxist ideology more than Christian doctrine. Moreover, Venezuela's current government is "leftist" and accused by the opposition of leading the country down a path to Communism.

Government supporters in Venezuela identify their president with former Chilean president Salvador Allende. In 1973, Allende was toppled by a U.S.-backed, right-wing coalition that mercilessly eliminated those they considered leftist sympathizers. This history is still alive in the collective conscience of Latin Americans. This lent weight to the pastor's concern for our team in the slums of the capital city.

The pastor's advice could be interpreted as gently steering us away from association with left-leaning pastors and Christian ministries. On the other hand, the openness and indirectness of his word left us with the freedom and responsibility to walk in the integrity of our convictions.

WHICH JESUS?

The pastor's surprising charge hounded me for answers. It wasn't clear to which Jesus we were to stick. The Jesus who "saved souls?" This was likely the Jesus the pastor had in mind. But what about the Jesus who broke the Sabbath laws in order to heal and restore the ostracized commoners? And the Jesus who dared to correct the power brokers of Israel? Do we stick to Jesus the soul-winning evangelist or to Jesus the revolutionary? One thing was certain. I knew that Jesus called us to stick to him as he stuck to the Father. In the words of John the evangelist, "As the Father sent me, so I send you." And so the search began.

JESUS THE RADICAL PROPHET

In the United States, growing numbers of Bible-believing Christians exhibit a deep conviction of a gospel for the poor. This is something to be grateful for. This group sees the world, and Scripture, through the lens of the struggle between social classes, between the rich and the poor. Inspiration for this comes from Old Testament prophets like Amos, who declared, "Let justice roll down like a river, and righteousness like a never-ending stream" (5:24). Exploitation by the rich is one of the reasons that Scripture gives for the existence of poverty. History, past and present, blatantly attests to this.

In light of this, we can stand up to injustice in the confidence that God is the foremost defender of the "widow and the orphan" and those who are opposed (Ps. 146). "Rich and poor" represents a lens through which we can read the Gospels. When we interpret Jesus' actions through this set of glasses, we end up with Jesus the radical prophet.

JESUS THE PERSONAL SAVIOR

Many Bible-believing Christians passionately preach the gospel wherever they can find an audience. This group stands on Jesus' own declaration that he came to "seek and save those who are lost." "Saving the lost," too, is a set of glasses through which we can read the Gospels. When we interpret Jesus' message through this lens, we end up with Jesus the personal Savior and soul winner. This Savior's overwhelming concern is proclamation and personal morality.

BLENDING THE TWO

My internal wrestling with the pastor's parting word reflects my experience of blending these Jesus portraits. This was no surprise since I am, with my InnerCHANGE co-workers, called to a ministry of proclaiming the gospel in word and demonstrating it through acts of justice.

At this point on my theological journey, help came in the form of a historical perspective from biblical scholar N. T. Wright.[1] I realized that in the search for answers, my thinking was stuck in a dead end. All I had managed to do was massage the soul-winning Jesus and the radical Jesus into a blend of the two. The result was good and encouraging as a perspective on what God is doing in today's church: the blended gospel breaks down the dividing line so that Christians don't have to choose between the two extremes. Yet I sensed that I hadn't gone far enough and that Scripture had more to say on the matter. This Jesus fell short of satisfying my quest.

BEYOND BLENDING

Wright helped me see that my categories were misconceived. I was reading the text through foreign lenses. I say "foreign" because "personal Savior" and "revolutionary" aren't titles used by the biblical writers themselves. These images don't emerge out of Israel's experience with their God. They were imposed on Scripture during later eras of church history.

Interpreting Jesus as I have—the radical who seeks justice for the poor and personal Savior who harvests individuals—didn't require me

---

1. Wright, *Challenge of Jesus*.

to understand the first century context of Israel. This alone should have signaled a warning that something had gone awry. I could detach the Jesus I worshiped on Sunday morning from the Jesus who walked the roads of Palestine. What Jesus' mission meant to his original audience was no concern to me when I considered how to reach out to my world today. My biblical interpretations could be characterized as free-floating or self-standing, without a foundation in the historical record of Jesus' original mission.

By approaching the Gospel accounts with these filters, I inadvertently forced Jesus to conform to *my* criteria. This inevitably created a Jesus who wasn't the Jesus of the Gospel narratives. Because this model lost its historical roots, it needed more than massaging. Its very frame needed to be realigned.

I resolved to let go of my satisfaction with simply blending the two Jesus images. I wanted to understand the Jesus who lived in the pages of the Gospels, in the historical context of first-century Palestine. Christ's mission within God's covenant history with Israel, therefore, became the starting point for my exploration. I resolved to interpret his mission through the Gospel narrative and the images and titles that emerged from it.

As a second step, the implications would surface for the contemporary context in which I live, the urban slums of Latin America. What follows is an overview of the historical perspective that shook the seismic plates of my interpretive foundation, furthering my quest to discover the Jesus to whom I'm called to stick.

ISRAEL'S (ONGOING) EXILE

Seven hundred years before Jesus' birth, God promised Israel that they would always have a king from David's lineage on the nation's throne (2 Sam 7). When the last two tribes lost their land to the Babylonians in 587 BC, Judah lost its king, and most Jews were taken captive to Babylon. This began what historians call Israel's exilic period. For seventy years, the nation lived with the tragic loss of the ancient signs (symbols) of God's covenant with them. These symbols served as tangible indicators that they were God's chosen people: the Torah (law), the temple, the land, and a Davidic king. The Torah was God's gift in the desert after saving them from Pharaoh's hand in Egypt. The promise of land was first pronounced to Israel's founding father, Abraham, through whom Yahweh promised to make Israel a great nation and a blessing to all the families of the earth.

After seventy years in captivity, a large percentage of Jews returned to their land, the land promised to them by Yahweh. Did this mark the end of Israel's exile? Those who returned to the land did manage to rebuild the temple, though not to its original glory. They rebuilt Jerusalem's wall. More importantly, they didn't reestablish a Davidic king or their sovereignty as a nation. Foreign powers continued to exercise political control over the land. The one remaining sign, not lost during this period, was the books of the Law. The people's adherence to the Law, therefore, took on renewed importance as the means for determining who belonged to the nation.

In the intervening years before the birth of Jesus, Israel's existence continued in a state of struggle to break free from foreign domination into the sovereignty and restoration they believed to be their God-given destiny as a nation. Their promised deliverance and restoration continually escaped their grasp. In a very real sense, the nation continued in exile, even while living in the Promised Land. Yahweh's promises remained unfulfilled, the signs of the covenant lost, and the nation's destiny in question.

GROWING EXPECTATIONS

In this extended period of turmoil and unrest, renewed expectations surfaced and gained momentum. Expectations mounted that a great and terrible day of God was coming—a day of restoration and judgment, of terror for Israel's enemies and vindication for God's elect. On that day, Yahweh himself would return to his people through his special messenger, the promised deliverer. Like Moses, he would lead the nation in a new exodus out of the bondage they suffered at the hands of the Babylonians, Medes, Persians, Syrians, and eventually the Romans. The annual Passover celebration reenacted this story of deliverance, which purveyed the hope that God would act yet again on their behalf.

Note the common theme of longing for that day of restoration and judgment, executed through the return of Yahweh to Zion.

> "See, I will send my messenger, who will prepare the way before me. Then suddenly the Lord you are seeking will come to his temple; the messenger of the covenant, whom you desire, will come," says the Lord Almighty. But who can endure the day of his coming? Who can stand when he appears? For he will be like a refiner's fire or a launderer's soap. He will sit as a refiner and purifier of silver; he will purify the Levites and refine them like gold and silver. Then the Lord will have men who will bring offerings in righteousness, and the offerings of Judah and Jerusalem will be acceptable to the Lord, as in days gone by, as in former years. So I will come near to you for judgment. I will be quick to testify against sorcerers, adulterers and perjurers, against those who defraud laborers of their wages, who oppress the widows and the fatherless, and deprive aliens of justice, but do not fear me," says the Lord Almighty. (Mal 3:1–5)
>
> "Surely the day is coming; it will burn like a furnace. All the arrogant and every evildoer will be stubble, and that day that is coming will set them on fire," says the Lord Almighty. "Not a root or a branch will be left to them. But for you who revere my name, the sun of righteousness will rise with healing in its wings. And you will go out and leap like calves released from the stall. Then you will trample down the wicked; they will be ashes under the soles of your feet on the day when I do these things," says the Lord Almighty. "Remember the law of my servant Moses, the decrees and laws I gave him at Horeb for all Israel. See, I will send you the prophet Elijah before that great and dreadful day of the Lord comes. He will turn the hearts of the fathers to their children, and the hearts of the children to their fathers; or else I will come and strike the land with a curse." (Mal 4:1–6)
>
> This is what the Lord says: "I will return to Zion and dwell in Jerusalem. Then Jerusalem will be called the City of Truth, and the mountain of the Lord Almighty will be called the Holy Mountain." This is what the Lord Almighty says: "Once again men and women of ripe old age will sit in the streets of Jerusalem, each with cane in hand because of his age. The city streets will be filled with boys and girls playing there." . . . "I will save my people from the countries of the east and the west. I will bring them back to live in Jerusalem; they will be my people, and I will be faithful and righteous to them as their God." (Zech 8:3–5, 7–8)

> Rejoice greatly, O Daughter of Zion!
> Shout, Daughter of Jerusalem!
> See, your king comes to you,
> righteous and having salvation,
> gentle and riding on a donkey,
> on a colt, the foal of a donkey.
> I will take away the chariots from Ephraim
> and the war-horses from Jerusalem,
> and the battle bow will be broken.
> He will proclaim peace to the nations.
> His rule will extend from sea to sea
> and from the River to the ends of the earth.
> As for you, because of the blood of my covenant with you,
> I will free your prisoners from the waterless pit. (Zech 9:9–11)
>
> On that day a fountain will be opened to the house of David and the inhabitants of Jerusalem, to cleanse them from sin and impurity. (Zech 13:1)

Israel's hope was greatly buoyed by the legacy of King David. Building on God's promise to an anointed shepherd boy (2 Sam 7), they clung to two deeply held expectations of what the coming king (the Messiah, the Anointed One, the Christ) would accomplish:

- the defeat of Israel's enemies (as David had done), and
- the building (or restoring) of the temple (as David's son, Solomon, had done).

In the meantime, how was the nation to remain true to their God and his law (Torah) while besieged on all sides by godless pagans? The people responded to this challenge by "sticking" to their God in a variety of ways:[2]

1. *Escaping* to the mountains to wait for the Day of the Lord (the Essenes)
2. *Fighting* against Rome, the pagan, gentile empire that occupied the land (the Zealots)
3. *Accommodating* to the ways of Rome and their political system (the Sadducees)
4. *Separating* from everything unclean and unworthy of Israel's identity as bearers of God's law (the scribes and Pharisees)

2. Ibid., 34–73.

In the face of centuries-long promises yet unfulfilled, God's people continued rising each morning to the probing question lodged in their ever-hopeful hearts: when will our God once again take up our cause and vindicate us as his special people? When will the day of our salvation come? When will God's deliverer come (like Moses or David) and take his rightful place?

No one, of course, knew when that day would come. The various factions most definitely disagreed on how God's salvation would arrive. Yet there was one thing on which they concurred. The day of the Lord would do away with Israel's oppressors as David had done with the Philistines and Moses with the Egyptians. In accomplishing this, God would renew the nation (and the nations!) in peace and justice around a gloriously reestablished temple.

SO WHAT?

Why did this historical perspective rock my interpretive foundation? Because it revealed the significance of the Savior's good news for first-century Israel and placed salvation within history, not simply in the sweet by-and-by. The people were awaiting God's vindication—the renewal of their nation, the re-establishment of their covenant signs, the fulfilling of God's promises, even the restoration of creation—before their pagan oppressors.

In a word, they expected their God to return, with all they believed that would entail. Jesus the Savior communicated unequivocally to Israel's well-attuned ear: "Yes! Your dream has come true! Your God has returned to his people! Your deliverer is here!"

If the message of Christ's mission wasn't that the day of the Lord had come, he wouldn't have proved such a threat to the Jewish authorities. But that's getting ahead of ourselves. As a prophet, Jesus carried out actions of justice that functioned as signs, or indicators, that *Israel's exile was finally over*. They pointed to the good news that Israel longed to hear. Their healing had come. God's promised forgiveness and restoration was revealed. Because Yahweh had returned, Jesus' message of repentance and faith was understood as turning from every way that promised God's vindication, to trust Jesus and the way he opened. All other paths would lead the nation to destruction.

As the fulfiller of God's promises to Israel, Jesus—Savior and prophet—became the new sign of God's faithfulness to the nation. This was his mission, in the simplest of terms. The implications of this calling, of course, were anything but simple, as we'll see.

5

My Enemy's Savior

FACING THE CLIFF ONLY a few feet away, Jesus saw his predicament. This was the decisive moment. He, the son of Joseph, turned and faced the angry crowd, the only way out of the quagmire. He walked, Scripture tells us, right through the mob of neighbors intent on pushing him over the edge.

Jesus . . . the deliverer and fulfiller of Yahweh's promises? If Jesus the Liberator's reception in Nazareth is any indication, his mission wasn't what Israel expected from their long-awaited King.

WHERE'S THE RUB?

On a recent Sunday, I heard a preacher argue that the offense of Jesus' ministry was his teaching on grace. Jesus, as he explained, preached justification by faith while the Pharisees and scribes preached justification by human merit. This exemplifies what I consider to be an interpretation divorced from the historical context of Jesus' mission to Israel—a reading that is foreign to the text, imported from a later era.

The conflict between faith and works, as commonly understood, wasn't the offense of Jesus' ministry. Israel had a long history of knowing God's grace, of being chosen by God. This doesn't mean that religiosity wasn't a problem. Yet God's undeserved saving acts didn't appear for the first time in the New Testament. The Old Testament chronicles Yahweh's graces bestowed upon the nation from its inception. The entire Bible, from Genesis to Revelation, testifies to God's unmerited mercy toward his creation.

Nor was the scandal of Jesus' message that he was presumably against the Law while the religious leaders defended it. Jesus wasn't against the Torah or its intent as a divine gift to Israel. He came to fulfill the law, not destroy it (Matt 5:22).

Another way this misunderstanding manifests itself is by pitting Israel's political agenda against Jesus' spiritual mission. This demarcation ignores the historical perspective I presented in chapter 4 that Israel's crisis was a covenant crisis—God's promises were unfulfilled, the signs of his covenant lost. This crisis, as we'll see, provides the key to understanding Jesus' good news to the nation and consequentially the nature of the gospel's offense.

Because Rome's occupation of the land painfully kept Israel's dilemma with God alive, ousting the oppressors from their territory represented political and spiritual restoration of their nation. These two dimensions could never be separated from each other. In a theocracy, as Israel was, these realms were inextricably woven together as one.

Even as I've argued that Israel awaited a salvation that would be political and spiritual, I would also propose that Christ's salvation was more than a narrowly-defined spiritual mission. According to Scripture, salvation is much more than imparting future assurances to individual souls. In fact, a robust biblical understanding of salvation will touch at least the following dimensions:

1. More than our souls get saved. The apostle Paul declared that our physical bodies will be redeemed (Rom 8:23). He knew this because he knew the resurrected Jesus, whose physical body was raised to new life on the third day. The transformation of our earthly bodies into heavenly bodies—as previewed in Jesus' nail-scarred hands and pierced side, which survived into the new realm—will not nullify the physicality of our existence but rather fulfill it, making us new (1 Cor 15:51–52; Rev 21:5).

2. God saves us into community. In creation, God made us male and female. In salvation, he reaches my neighbor and me. Love for God and neighbor are indivisibly held together. Not loving the one we see reveals that we don't love God, the One we cannot see (1 John 4:20–21). Finding peace with God is coupled with finding peace with our neighbor (Matt 22:37), the second commandment "resembling" the first. In the prodigal parable, the older son's reconciliation with the father is linked to his reconciliation with his brother. The younger brother in turn is restored to the village community

through the father's party, a celebration of and a testimony to the salvation wrought by the father. In the epistles, Paul calls the church to be the "new man," reflecting the apostle's vision of God's people as renewed humans walking in the knowledge of God's image.

3. The physical earth gets saved, too. God's creation was "good" from the beginning and will be "made new" (Isa 65:17–25; 2 Pet 3:12; Rev 21–22) and "liberated" on the day of redemption (Rom 8:21–23).

4. Our "good works" on earth "survive" (1 Cor 3:14). Jesus' "good work" of dying on the cross for us survived in his resurrected body, as his nail-scarred hands and pierced side testify. In a highly eschatological passage, Paul names things such as knowledge, prophesy, and tongues that will *not* last beyond this age. In contrast to this, faith, hope, and love remain to the time when "we shall see face to face" (1 Cor 13:12–13).

Each of these points merits further attention, which I endeavor to do in subsequent chapters. For now, suffice it to say that we can't limit the reach of God's reign to a spiritual realm that ignores the physical, social, material, and economic dimensions of the world God created. The kingdom announced by Christ is eternal and true: it is the in-breaking of God's loving, redemptive authority. In small, seed-like fashion, the reconstituting of Israel through his twelve disciples marked Jesus' way of harvesting the first fruits of a new world, God's renewed humanity. Embedded in Jesus' kingdom message and mission was the DNA of a salvation that leavens all of life and creation, even if only in embryonic form.

Why did the authorities get so upset? Having read the Gospels through the optic of Jesus the personal Savior for many years, I remember all too well that nagging sense I would have after reading and rereading the Jesus narratives. Something didn't add up. Jesus' message of grace didn't explain their rage. I was left with a gnawing sense that I was missing an essential element of the story.

Could the radical-prophet optic help? According to this view, Jesus broke social taboos. He fraternized with the wrong crowd, touching those who were untouchable. He included those who were socially excluded by the traditions and institutions the authorities upheld. This was deeply offensive to the Jewish leaders because it revealed their arrogance and unfaithfulness to God's higher laws of love. This dimension of Jesus' conduct was clearly offensive. Yet this kind of reasoning left me dissatisfied. Would Jesus' unbridled love and acceptance of people considered unclean and unworthy be so offensive to warrant eliminating him? I didn't think so.

The gospel's offense only started to make sense when I considered it within its historical setting, as I'll try to demonstrate in two interpretive samplings from the Gospel of Mark.

REVISITING THE OLD, OLD STORY

Mark 2:2–12: A Clash of Authorities

> So many gathered that there was no room left, not even outside the door, and he preached the word to them. Some men came, bringing to him a paralytic, carried by four of them. Since they could not get him to Jesus because of the crowd, they made an opening in the roof above Jesus and, after digging through it, lowered the mat the paralyzed man was lying on. When Jesus saw their faith, he said to the paralytic, "Son, your sins are forgiven." Now some teachers of the law were sitting there, thinking to themselves, "Why does this fellow talk like that? He's blaspheming! Who can forgive sins but God alone?" Immediately Jesus knew in his spirit that this was what they were thinking in their hearts, and he said to them, "Why are you thinking these things? Which is easier: to say to the paralytic, 'Your sins are forgiven,' or to say, 'Get up, take your mat and walk'? But that you may know that the Son of Man has authority on earth to forgive sins . . ." He said to the paralytic, "I tell you, get up, take your mat and go home." He got up, took his mat and walked out in full view of them all. This amazed everyone and they praised God, saying, "We have never seen anything like this!"

Doesn't this story confirm that the main point of Jesus' mission was the forgiveness of sins, and that we in turn follow him for the personal Savior that he is? Then again, the narrative also points to Jesus the radical prophet who offered an unencumbered welcome, complete with spiritual and physical freedom, to an outsider. Let's look closer.

Jesus offered God's forgiveness to the paralytic. The scribes reacted immediately. They were offended by the audacity of Jesus to pronounce such a thing. In their response, they were correct to attribute their sense of violation of God and his right alone to forgive sins. Yet how were sins forgiven in Israel? By whom? And under what circumstances? Were there barriers that the system erected that prevented people from receiving forgiveness and acceptance in the community?

Forgiveness Back Then

The scribes, as experts in the Torah, were stewards of the socio-religious rules and protocol for granting forgiveness of sins and cancellation of debts. This power made them gatekeepers of the community. Anyone needing to pass from the condition of indebtedness, culpability, or impurity to a condition of freedom from indebtedness, guilt, or purity had to pass through the scribes' careful eye for the prescribed temple rituals. As a doctor today diagnoses a patient, so the scribes and priests had the recognized role and authority to diagnose who was in proper standing (in every sense of that word—spiritually, socially, etc.). They controlled what was needed to put things right.

In Venezuela, citizen identification cards are central to daily life. Without my government-issued ID card, my children can't attend school. Nor can I get a job or receive government assistance. Imagine the vast majority of Venezuelans without this all-important ID card. Then a charismatic community leader comes along and gives the poor ID numbers and all the corresponding rights. Imagine him doing this without government authorization. Needless to say, this would be scandalous, not to mention a serious violation of the law. The obvious question would be, who gave this grassroots figure the authority to hand out ID cards? This is how Jesus' authority to forgive must have been perceived by Israel's leaders.

The matter of forgiveness brought to light a clash of symbols, old and new. The teachers of the law believed that the authority to forgive rested in two ancient symbols in Israel: the Law (Torah) and the temple. As scribes they were stewards of these God-ordained signs of the covenant. Yet Jesus granted forgiveness without regard for the scribes' role and the authority of Torah laws and temple traditions. To act as if he were the new sign was unacceptable and offensive beyond our imagination. To top it off, he sealed his word of forgiveness with a healing command that brought the disabled man to his feet.

The Unacceptable Authority Assumed by Jesus

By forgiving people, Jesus acted as if he were the true temple and the ultimate authority. The teachers of the law were, not surprisingly, offended that he assumed an authority greater than even the Torah. What a heresy! With this action, Jesus treated the signs and symbols of God's covenant people as unnecessary. For Jesus to insist he stood taller than the temple and the Torah, which God himself had ordained, was an abomination. The leaders believed that, if left alone, this preacher-prophet and his growing crowd of followers represented a serious threat to the nation as it was constituted.

The main point of this story wasn't that God forgives and Jesus came to forgive sins (in an ahistorical sense). Nor was it that Jesus came to restore the dignity of those who are excluded and rejected. Don't get me wrong—these dimensions of Jesus' work were essential to what he came to do. I'm arguing that they must be understood in relation to the more fundamental truth to which the narrative points. The heart of the matter was that Israel's time of desolation was over. The day of the Lord had arrived. God's true and eternal temple had come and their sin was forgiven. God's promises, including the Law itself, were being fulfilled in the person and the mission of Jesus.

Mark 2:14–17: A Scandalous Glimpse at Israel's Future

> As he walked along, Jesus saw Levi son of Alphaeus sitting at the tax collector's booth. "Follow me," Jesus told him, and Levi got up and followed him. While Jesus was having dinner at Levi's house, many tax collectors and "sinners" were eating with him and his disciples, for there were many who followed him. When the teachers of the law who were Pharisees saw him eating with the "sinners" and tax collectors, they asked his disciples: "Why does he eat with tax collectors and 'sinners'?" On hearing this, Jesus said to them, "It is not the healthy who need a doctor, but the sick. I have not come to call the righteous, but sinners."

If Jesus had been a respectable Jewish leader, he wouldn't have shared table fellowship with those considered impure and indebted. Yet Jesus accepted people that the system excluded. He audaciously gave privileged status to sinners. He even declared that to be the reason why he came. Jesus subverted the elders' laws and traditions.

Christians of the radical, revolutionary Jesus stop here in their reading of the gospel, since up to this point a Marxist, class-struggle interpretation stands on biblical ground. (The "last will be first . . ."; the "foolish shame the wise"; God "fills the hungry, but sends the rich away empty.") Yet the weight of the passage rests elsewhere, and the audacity of Jesus goes even further.

In this meal we see a sign of the new covenant that Jesus was inaugurating. Eating with sinners dramatically declared to the authorities of Israel: *This is the future of our nation! With the authority of my heavenly father, I'm taking Israel to its God-given destiny according to the promises of her God. You're witnessing a faithful testimony to the covenant as the Almighty designed it from the beginning, now made new in me. The day of the Lord is here! Those who receive the good news of their healing and restoration are the "sick" who take their place at the banquet of the renewed Israel! Blessed are those who see this and believe!*

Jesus didn't break the rules for the sake of being a radical in defense of the poor. Nor did he do so to reform the system or to be an example of evangelizing the rejected. Jesus broke the rules of the prevailing order to demonstrate and fulfill Israel's mission. This explains why the authorities considered Jesus a heretic and a deceiver, and why he caused such great concern. His popularity posed a serious problem. But how could they allow someone with such a distorted vision for the nation deceive the ignorant masses?

I see the prodigal's father in this. Like the conflict between the father and his older son, the conflict between Jesus and Israel's leaders was inevitable because Israel's understanding was too small. The point wasn't the restoration of one nation (or one son!). It was something much bigger: God's kingdom coming for all nations (both sons!). The conflicts resulted from Jesus demonstrating that bigger future. Jesus' actions were an offensive vision of God's future for humankind. That vision asked more of Israel than they were willing to give.

WHO PUSHED WHOM OVER THE EDGE?

Think back to the cliffhanger episode in Luke 4:16–30. Jesus so deeply offended the members of the synagogue in his hometown of Nazareth that they tried to throw him over a cliff. This story baffled me for years. It made no sense when approached with the lens of Jesus the personal Savior or Jesus the radical prophet.

Why didn't Jesus stop after his initial announcement? He had declared in essence, "I'm the Anointed one, the coming King. The day of the Lord has come, and your desolation is over. Believe the Good News!" Were the people offended by Jesus making the poor his priority? Hardly, since many of them were probably poor. They were likely a bit starstruck by their local boy-made-good. In any event, they welcomed the day of the Lord's favor for Israel.

It seems to me Jesus knew they didn't understand the fullness of his message, so he pressed further. "There were many widows in Israel at the time of Elijah . . . and many lepers in the time of Elisha . . . yet the prophets were not sent to them. They were sent to the widows and lepers beyond Israel." Jesus' mission included the older *and* the younger son. By drawing the synagogue worshipers into these familiar stories, Jesus surprised them with a radically different interpretation of Israel's promised messiah. Israel expected their messiah to defeat their enemies. According to the prevailing assumption at the time, the biggest hindrance to the day of the Lord was the Roman presence, their foreign occupiers. They were the enemies the Davidic king would defeat.

With these highly-charged words, Jesus declared from Israel's own story, "The problem is not your gentile neighbors. And the solution is not to war against your enemies in God's name. Remember my promise to your father Abraham and my intentions from the beginning to bless, not curse, all nations. This is *my* promise and *your* purpose."

Israel had absolutized their nationalism. Jesus rightly assumed a posture of relativity toward his people. (Note that I don't mean he was dispassionate toward Israel!) He called the townspeople to the same, to step out of their idolatrous self-identity and to submit to Jesus' primacy over both Jew and gentile.

Did they understand Jesus' message at that point? Their rage seems to indicate they understood him quite well. The kingdom would mean a new relationship to the world beyond their ethnic borders—that is, with their gentile neighbors. It would also mean a new relationship with their God, expressed in a new covenant.

I see my brother Caligallo in this. In the violent slums of Caracas, God would say, "Your problem is not the Caligallos of the neighborhood, and the solution to your crisis is not to violently take revenge against the street criminals." Caligallo was no Christ figure. He was a street criminal. He was also a child of God. Jesus was the Christ, God's promised deliverer. Yet he was also "counted among thieves," a violator of Israel's traditions, a genuine threat to his neighborhood. The kingdom coming to the slums must mean, at the very least, a new relationship to the world beyond one's own family and those considered safe and worthy.

MORE THAN A PRINCIPLE

I see a thread running through the Gospel narratives, the prodigal parable, and the drama of Caligallo's death. I suspect that it's much weightier than a thread. What I'm referring to isn't the offense of the gospel itself, which I've already begun unpacking. I see a particular hue that this offense takes, an edge to it that makes it truly cutting.

The offense is never abstract.[1] The dutiful son sees the implications for himself. As the older sibling, he'll have to follow his father's example and accept his brother back into the family. He doesn't want to change, and there's no way to sidestep the issue. It's a family affair. If he could negotiate the matter, he would no doubt take the father without his little brother. (Things were going quite well actually while the little runt was gone, thank you very much.) Yet the father makes it clear that a divided, incomplete family isn't an option. Thus the offense.

The gospel's offense wasn't due to the violation of a principle. The personal Savior we've created, who preaches grace over works and spiritual over political, is a Savior who overturns a principle. He declares, in essence, "I stand for this, not that." His followers, you and me, either agree or disagree. Yet we don't experience direct implications for ourselves. The clash remains abstract and distant. It doesn't touch us.

The same holds for the followers of Jesus the radical prophet. We either agree or disagree with this prophet's posture towards the least and the last. Such a revolutionary attracts us, or he doesn't. Yet we don't experience the implications of his actions personally. From a distance we consider what he's done and whether we're impressed by it or not.

In my slum, the Caligallo problem, if I may put it that way, was and continues to be a personal issue for everyone. To not condemn him represents an irresponsible posture that endangers the neighborhood. The gospel challenge to see street criminals as human beings worthy of an equal chance to experience God's saving grace comes with a knife-

---

1. Ellul, *Presence of Kingdom*, 49–78.

sharp edge. Extending grace could spell the end for me. It could cost me my life.

THE CROSS ANTICIPATED

Returning to the drama at the cliff's edge, yet with the prodigal and Caligallo in the shadows, we see something else in the rage of the synogogue: the cross. For the offense that occurred in Luke 4 grew, becoming an earth-shaking crescendo at Calvary. In other words, what they did to Christ on the cross is what they did to him each step of the way. Therefore, Jesus dramatized from the beginning the costly love he displayed at the end. Kenneth Bailey aptly describes this continuity as "costly demonstrations of unexpected love"[2] carried throughout the Messiah's ministry and culminating at Golgatha. I liken this to the cross quietly inserting itself at each juncture of the gospel narrative like a treasure half-hidden along the rocky path.

The thick stage curtain is getting pulled back and the pastor's haunting advice answered. The Savior to whom I stick is the One who offensively fulfilled God's promises. Like a strong, loving father, he loved me and my adversary at great personal cost.

---

2. Bailey, *Jesus through Middle Eastern Eyes*, 180, 236.

6

At the Cliff's Edge

> I laid a foundation as an expert builder, and someone else is building on it. But each one should be careful how he builds. For no one can lay any foundation other than the one already laid, which is Jesus Christ. (1 Cor 3:10–11)

Jesus, our Lord and Savior, was the offensive fulfiller of God's promised kingdom. The parable of the prodigal paints our scandalous Deliverer in the vivid hues of a father who runs and pleads for his lost sons. This Savior and prophet is Lord of rich and poor, friend and foe, sinner and saint, Jew and gentile. He is the one and only foundation upon which we, the Church, are built—an unchanging foundation because he is a person who lived and acted in history.

Though the essence of our faith is inherited from those who have gone before us, the task of understanding the foundation belongs to every generation that encounters the living Christ and his Good News. It is never frozen in time, simply handed down through the centuries.

Paul described his efforts as that of an expert builder, one who understood the foundation. He charged those who built upon the foundation to do so with care. That is my intent—that we carefully consider the foundation and how we are building. For we build ministries according to how we see the foundation.

Those who lay a foundation of Jesus as personal Savior develop ministries that prioritize proclamation—often with a highly individualized message. Those who follow Jesus the radical prophet develop ministries of social significance that prioritize the place of the poor in God's kingdom, and the importance of our role as change agents. Variations of these formulations abound. What is at stake in our reexamination of the foundation is nothing less than the nature of our witness, which obviously rests, not inconsequentially, upon our image of God.

OUR FOUNDATION IS AT THE CLIFF'S EDGE[1]

> See I lay a stone in Zion, a chosen and precious cornerstone, and the one who trusts in him will never be put to shame. Now to you who believe, this stone is precious. But to those who do not believe, the stone the builders rejected has become the cornerstone, and a stone that causes men to stumble and a rock that makes them fall. (1 Pet 2:6–8, citing Isa 8:14; 28:16; Ps 118:22)

The dramatic episode of Jesus' announcement in his hometown of Nazareth (Luke 4:16–30) demonstrates from the very beginning of his public ministry that he would be "a sign that will be spoken against, so that the thoughts of many hearts will be revealed" (Luke 2:34–35). What better description for what transpired at the cliff's edge? Our cornerstone, Jesus Christ, became our foundation through rejection and persecution. His mission was offensive to "the builders," causing them to "stumble." Becoming the cornerstone through such scandal was a surprise act. No one saw it coming.

In Nazareth, Jesus pushed his fellow Jews to the edge by implying that they would have to share God's blessing with pagan neighbors and become family with their enemies. In turn, they literally forced Jesus out of town. Three years later, on the cross, Jesus our foundation is found "outside the gate" again! He committed his final and greatest act of righteousness and restoration in the most unexpected, dramatic, and costly fashion yet. With a crescendolike effect that culminated in Roman execution, he bore the sin and ridicule of those who rejected the audacity of God's far-reaching forgiveness and reconciliation.

UNDERSTATING OUR DIFFICULTY WITH GOD

It's risky to stick to this scandalous Jesus. It inevitably leads us to unlikely people and places where we listen to those of different color, creed, gender, and political agenda. It is unpopular with those who are guardians

---

1, González, *Santa Biblia*, 31–55.

of the prevailing absolutized views. If we don't see the dangers, we're not seeing this for what it is.

Scripture is even more forceful in its depiction of the gospel as a stumbling block: "This child is destined to cause the falling and rising of many in Israel, and to be a sign that will be spoken against, so that the thoughts of many hearts will be revealed. And a sword will pierce your own soul too" (Luke 2:34–35). Through Simeon, the Holy Spirit prepared Mary for the scandal that lay ahead for her child, that Israel's rejection of their Messiah would lead to great suffering. "You stiff-necked people . . . you have betrayed and murdered him—you who have received the law . . . but have not obeyed it" (Acts 7:51–53). "Like one from whom men hide their faces he was despised, and we esteemed him not" (Isa 53:3).

It's no wonder that his neighbors in Nazareth tried to throw Jesus over the cliff. He placed himself and God's day of fulfillment beyond the borders of the nation with Israel's enemies and called them to follow him there. Impossible! Absurd! Moreover, if the ignorant masses swallowed this preacher's message, the nation itself would be lost.

DO WE HAVE EYES TO SEE?

> For the message of the cross is foolishness to those who are perishing, but to us who are being saved it is the power of God . . . we preach Christ crucified: a stumbling block to Jews and foolishness to gentiles . . . not many of you were of noble birth. But God chose the foolish things of this world to shame the wise . . . we speak of God's secret wisdom, a wisdom that has been hidden . . . God has revealed it to us by his Spirit . . . we have the mind of Christ. (1 Cor 1:18, 23; 2:7, 10, 16)

Humbling myself enough to reconcile with an undeserving person looks foolish, according to the apostle. I don't like to make myself vulnerable to someone who has hurt me or with whom I deeply disagree. Yet Paul seemed to know Jesus the Savior, who runs to the wayward, and Jesus the prophet, who patiently pleads with the stubbornly civilized.

In this scenario of foolishness I see Corrie in the hospital extending her hand of forgiveness to Caligallo, the orphan-gone-bad. I see Ryan with his friend Chris praying in Caligallo's shack overlooking the precipice. Nor can I forget my friend José with fruit in hand, against the warnings of his wife, daring to approach Caligallo the hated killer. Finally, I see myself challenged by the God of shalom who is outside the party, pleading with me, calling me—even when my resistance to bless the manipulating politicians of Washington, whom I can blame for my dad's premature death, pushes him to the cliff's edge. What a foolishly loving God we worship! And what a scandalously challenging mission we receive!

Part 2
Partners at Cornelius' House

Typical Venezuelan altar

7

Spiritual Power Encountered

"Señor Juan (John), Blanca and Daniel need your help, their nephew has a bad spirit."

My team was concluding day four of an eight-day missionary training event in the neighborhood. Things were going quite well. It was 9:00 p.m. I looked forward to relaxing at the end of a stimulating day, not tackling "bad spirits."

Blanca and Daniel's little one-room brick shack was built in the already-tiny back patio of the house that my family rented. The Cuban doctor assigned to serve the community was leaving as I arrived. He had determined that German, the sixteen-year-old young man, was not sick. Nor was he drunk.

When I stepped into the room, German went into a violent trance, shaking all over. He frothed at the mouth, and his pupils turned upward and out of sight. At times he calmed down only to fly out of control without warning, tossing and turning on the bed, which filled half of the dwelling.

Daniel and another man were out of their minds—yelling at each other, yelling at German, frantically sitting on top of him, doing everything within their physical strength to subdue him. They slapped him in the face, shook him, and threw themselves upon him to somehow bring him to. They clearly expected me, the resident "man of God," to take care of the situation. I knew with one look at the young man that I had never encountered a case of demonization like this.

I had no idea what to do. I sat at the bedside stalling for time. Fortunately, my teammate Steve and a Venezuelan believer showed up. In the name of Jesus they silenced the demon, who had been controlling German's voice. With some effort, they got German's attention. They invited him to exercise his will in an act of renouncing the demon and receiving Christ into his life. German complied. God's peace reigned and the dark episode ended.

I rejoined the missionary trainees, still gathered in the meeting hall, feeling incapable of talking about what had happened. I felt exposed and embarrassed. I, the missionary trainer, couldn't deal with demons. How could I prepare others for missionary service without being prepared myself?

MEETING MR. O

Three years later, nearly five years into our work in Caracas, I made a house visit that forever changed me. I met the man who would reorient me, the man who would educate me about the spirit world of Venezuelans.

Mr. O was a grieving father. Four young men had ripped their enemy—Mr. O's son—out of bed in the middle of the night, tied him up, and shot him in cold blood. I made my first of many visits to Mr. O the next day. At the time I saw the visit as a straightforward though difficult house call. I didn't know that the sagely, bedridden man of nearly sixty years with pencil-thin limbs and dark, African features would become my teacher. Though I encountered a grieving father, I also came face to face with a man consumed with manipulating the spirit world to get revenge on the killers of his two sons. (Another son had been murdered two years before.) What began with listening to his grief became, over time, a deep and sometimes clashing exchange of faiths and practices.

In Venezuela the line blurs between what is called sorcery, witchcraft, spiritism, and even Santería.[1] Venezuelans are often spiritually eclectic, borrowing symbols, methods, and deities freely among the vast array of folk spiritualities and religions. Mr. O sees visions in cigar smoke, reads tobacco leaves, and receives visitations from "Lucifer." He uses the "orishas" (the seven African deities of Santería) for protection and has a home altar with the Venezuelan goddess, María Lionza, at its head. Mr. O also uses black magic to eliminate those responsible for his sons' deaths. He literally gives my teammates and me updates on how many have "fallen," or if he sees their end in sight.

---

1. Pollak-Eltz, *Religiosidad Popular*, 13–29.

He sometimes laments the legacy of violence that he's leaving his children and grandchildren, insisting that nothing can change. We typically share a Gospel story or a passage on the teaching of God's kingdom. Deep mutual respect, laughter, personal sharing, and a cup of coffee mark every visit. When he realizes that following the Jesus who forgave his killers would mean renouncing the witchcraft that fuels his vengeful heart, the gospel conversations come to a screeching halt.

Though I had encountered German, the demonized young man three years before, it wasn't until my encounter with Mr. O that I was ready to face my deficiencies in three critical areas: my lack of experience with demonized people; my secularized gospel that, in practice, didn't believe in the spirit world; and my lack of spiritual power as a Christian.

THE CHALLENGE OF CHANGING

Almost immediately, the Lord began moving on the first two matters. One afternoon my wife, Birgit, became uncharacteristically distraught. She and I sensed that her level of anxiety went beyond what she normally experienced. We took time to discern and pray. I didn't pray a general prayer, asking God to set her free. I took authority, in Jesus' name, commanding the spirit that we had identified to leave. For days afterward, Birgit testified to a profound release she experienced as a result of this prayer.

Curiously, fifteen years earlier, I encountered something similar. We worked among Central Americans in the inner city of Los Angeles, California. Our eighteen-month-old daughter, Marna, awoke in the middle of the night, terribly distraught, wailing at the top of her lungs. Every attempt to ease her pain failed. Finally, as a last, desperate effort, I stepped out on a limb against my natural instincts and exercised Christ's authority in prayer, commanding the tormenting spirit to go. In the most dramatic fashion, Marna experienced immediate release from what had been causing her pain.

WHAT INNER-CITY L.A. TRIED TO TEACH ME

While serving in the inner city of Los Angeles, California in the '90s, I witnessed other unusual works of the Holy Spirit. I knew a troubled teenager named Tomás, whose commitment to Christ was plagued by deep personal issues. His problems, in my mind, provided ample reason why God would never entrust him with exceptional spiritual power. One evening in 1994 Tomás attended a "revival meeting" in Pasadena, California where Christians on fire with the "Toronto blessing" held nightly meetings. Tomás came back in a laughing fit that lasted a week. During those days he sat on our living room couch in stitches, bubbling over with joy. Struggling to contain his laughter enough to speak, he managed to interrupt it long enough to verbalize what I can only describe as Old Testament oracles. Lengthy Bible passages came out of his mouth one after the other—Scriptures that Tomás had never read, much less committed to memory.

In another incident on Christmas Eve two years later, we invited a handful of loners to spend the evening with us. Georgeanne was one of them. She lived alone in a single-room-occupancy hotel across the street that catered to the transient population. Georgeanne had mental limitations. Unable to work, she lived from a monthly government check. The teachers at the local adult learning center took pity on her by admitting her each year as a student. Georgeanne, a Caucasian, stood out among the many Latino, Korean, and Japanese students. Her pre-adolescent mind and childlike demeanor lived in a three-hundred-pound body. On graduation day each year, she mounted the stage, held up a tiny American flag she found at the 99-cent store, and performed a jig to the tune of "The Star Spangled Banner"—and the jeers of her less-than-admiring classmates.

Shortly before the Christmas season, a Korean church took Georgeanne under their wing. She experienced family with them. Because of what Georgeanne learned from her new church, she knew exactly what to do when she arrived and found our son, John Mark (two years old at the time), suffering from an ear infection. My youngest child lay on the couch, immobile and sickly.

Georgeanne approached him, put her hands on his ears and commanded, "You devils, get out of John Mark's ears!" That was it. Quite simple. Within a couple minutes the next guest showed up at the door. To my amazement John Mark bounced off the couch, ran to the door, and hid behind it to surprise the visitor. My son was healed. Every symptom of the ear infection vanished, including his fever and achy muscles.

In spite of this, my worldview didn't change. One experience with the demonic didn't outweigh a lifetime of not believing in the work of demons. At that juncture in my journey, I stood on the threshold of a profound change in my basic assumptions about the world. But I did *not* step through the door. I stepped back, essentially unchanged. Now, years later, after seeing the freedom experienced by my wife, I stood once again looking through the same threshold.

Within weeks my sixteen-year-old daughter had a freak asthma attack at 2:00 a.m. She sat in the bathroom, arms and legs flailing uncontrollably. I knew from experience that her behavior went beyond what was normal. I discerned that a demonic presence was taking advantage of her physical condition, making it worse and preventing me from helping her. I took authority in Jesus' name, commanding the spirit to release her. Johanna's legs and arms fell limp. We could then address her breathing difficulties.

Later, our middle daughter, thirteen at the time, confessed to me while putting her to bed one night, "Dad, after downloading a music video from the internet, I sensed that it wasn't from God. It feels like something attached to my head . . . right here." She pointed to the back side of her head. We talked about what it could be. We discerned that it could be a spirit of darkness. After commanding the spirit of darkness to leave, my daughter experienced complete physical and spiritual release.

Not to be left out, my son surprised me with intense weeping at bedtime. I assumed it must have been provoked by his sadness over the farewell of a dear friend. Yet what he said startled me: "I'm so confused, Dad. What will happen to me when I die?" His sobbing continued unabated.

Pop psychologist that I am, I inquired, "Are you sad about Ryan leaving?" "No, Dad. I'm confused! I don't know what will happen to me when I die." After probing a little more, I asked my son if he was okay with me praying against a possible spirit of confusion. With little fanfare, my son experienced genuine freedom from the spirit of confusion that was troubling him.

WORLDVIEW INSIGHTS

My formation within a secular worldview didn't prepare me to see the work of demons. I assumed that efforts to help the hurting through demonic deliverance discouraged personal responsibility. This need not be. Professor Charles Kraft likens demons to rats that feed off garbage. Demons need to cling to something. Issues of sin, personal wounds, and moments of trauma provide gateways for destructive spirits to latch on and worsen a person's condition.[2]

Not only was I ill-prepared to recognize demons, I discovered (yet again!) just how syncretistic my understanding of the Good News was. I stood guilty of teaching a secularized gospel (see chart below).

The Secular-Animistic Axis[3]		
Secularism The belief that there are no spiritual powers.	Biblical theism The conception of God as sovereign over his world while allowing people the freedom to choose their allegiances.	Animism The view that the world is largely controlled by spiritual forces and that human beings must manipulate these unseen powers.

This jolting revelation came with an equally poignant realization that my neighbors lean in the other direction. Venezuela is highly animistic in orientation. It's quite normal for Venezuelans to appeal to spirits to resolve their problems. They believe the basic disposition of God and these lesser beings is *not* favorable toward humans. Therefore, they

---

2. Kraft, *Christianity with Power*, 26–49.
3. Van Rheenen, *Communicating Christ in Animistic Contexts*, 96.

must barter and make promises to get what they need. If they don't get what they ask for, they look for another, more favorable spiritual source.

Venezuelan intermediaries include, José Gregorio Hernandez, a deeply venerated medical doctor who served the poor selflessly at the turn of the twentieth century, and María Lionza, a goddess with special powers over nature. According to legend, she was the daughter of an Indian chief. Her statue stands prominently in the middle of the main freeway through Caracas and portrays her with the strength of an indigenous resistance figure. The cult of María Lionza is a spirituality that changes and adapts to the times, incorporating new deities as needed.

The mountain Sorte, in the Venezuelan state of Yaracuy, a sacred place of pilgrimage, attracts countless María Lionza devotees year round, especially on October 12. The goddess is head deity among Venezuela's three powers, a functioning trinity that includes the Indian Guaicaipuro and the slave Negro Primero.

The "orishas" of Santería also act as intermediaries. Unlike the María Lionza cult, Santería is a formalized religion with an established set of beliefs. It comes from the Yoruba people of Nigeria (known there as Lukumi). Exported to Cuba through slaves, it mixed with Catholicism then spread through the Caribbean. In Venezuela, it's experiencing a resurgence. Growing numbers of men, women and children don the white, whole-body attire and the corresponding necklaces and bracelets of first-year apprentices.

WHAT SEMINARY TRIED TO TEACH ME

> I studied at Fuller Theological Seminary in Pasadena, California when a controversial course, "Church Growth and Signs and Wonders" taught by John Wimber, was discontinued. The course brought into conflict the institution and the work of the Spirit while deeply impacting two professors of mission, Charles Kraft and Peter Wagner.
>
> Because of the palpable hunger among the students for more of the Spirit's power, Dr. Kraft and Dr. Wagner negotiated a settlement with the seminary. As an alternative to the course itself, they lined up teachers to conduct a non-credit class on Monday evenings. I attended each session. I was exposed to a deeper understanding of the Holy Spirit in a positive and safe

environment where people of little background or experience could explore and learn. For whatever reason, I didn't jump in with both feet.

Curiously, an oft-heard refrain from mission professors was that they ministered in the developing world twenty years without appreciating the people's understanding of the spirit world. This enormous blind spot hampered every aspect of their work, representing probably their greatest regret. Deeply impressed by these testimonies, I took them to heart as "important lessons learned in seminary." I sincerely believed myself immune to such error.

HELP OF A DIFFERENT KIND

These lessons convinced me that I needed more of God's power to minister in this environment. For this reason we invited a man named Bob Ekblad to come and minister to our team. In the mornings, Bob and his teammate Chris ministered to us. We were all touched in different ways. One team member received the gift of tongues. Another experienced a deep wave of tears that God used to shower his love on her. Others experienced God's healing touch in their bodies. We also made house visits to read the Bible and pray for the sick.

The evening after they left, I remember saying goodnight to Johanna, my sixteen-year-old daughter. She asked me straight out: "Dad, will things go back to the way they were?" I knew what she meant. She and her siblings experienced God's powerful presence through Bob's ministry. At my daughter's bedside, I confess I didn't possess great faith. I wasn't certain. In spite of my doubts, I found myself saying, "No. Things will be different."

During the week that followed, I felt discouraged. Things did seem like before. I didn't sense anything special. A week after Bob and Chris left, we gathered for team prayer. After an opening prayer, I struck the first chord of a song on my guitar to lead the team in worship. With the first strum of my instrument, my hands started burning. Within seconds, my arms were consumed with the fiery sensation. It felt like a deep, electrical charge. I barely made it through the first song as my hands and arms became increasingly immobile. I laid the guitar aside and slid out of my chair to the floor.

For the next four hours my teammates attended to me on the floor as I was fully consumed by the fiery presence of God. They pulled out my journal and took notes as I spoke out visions and messages that I sensed God giving me. They prayed over me, also speaking inspired messages of what God seemed to be showing them. This happened every Tuesday morning in team prayer for the next five weeks, though the experiences were somewhat shorter.

NO TURNING BACK

Shortly after Bob Ekblad's visit, Birgit and I met with a woman named Yuri in a nearby slum area. Yuri was not a believer, and we had read Scripture with her on one or two occasions. Her reputation in the neighborhood was not flattering, and her home life was a disaster. On this particular day we sensed God at work, opening her heart a bit to the Lord. At one point in the conversation Yuri expressed a genuine concern for her marriage, asking us to pray for her and her husband.

When I extended my hand toward her in prayer, a frightening spirit jerked her around, contorting her face and speaking through her mouth in a blood-curdling voice: "She's mine . . . she's mine . . . she's mine." From the little we'd learned at that point in our experience with demons, we exercised Christ's authority to silence it and then expel it. Within a few minutes, the episode concluded with Yuri set free, delivered from the tormenting demon.

The following week she testified to us, "Before you prayed for me, I constantly heard voices telling me, 'Leave your family,' 'Go to the streets.' From my front door I saw a cemetery when I looked down the hill. Now I look out over my slum and see the homes."

Soon after this experience with Yuri, I told some friends about it. They weren't from Yuri's slum, nor did they know her. They couldn't get information directly from her. I simply told them the name of the spirit and they replied, "We know that spirit too. It's the one that a woman uses against another woman

> when she wants to steal their husband. It's a spirit that destroys marriages. It's probably behind 70 percent of the divorces in Venezuela." Were we missionaries the only ones who didn't "know" this spirit?
>
> In that moment, I knew my worldview, and my ministry, would never be the same. Sadly, Yuri wasn't willing to follow the One who set her free, and has reopened herself to even worse spirits. The spirit dimensions of ministry never seemed so real to me.

During the summer after Bob's visit, I noticed a buzzing sensation in my right hand. I thought it might be a pinched nerve. I went for a massage, thinking that might loosen up the tightness from my neck. Yet the low-grade buzzing in my hand was sometimes in my feet and upper chest. Whenever I turned my mind to the Lord or called on Jesus in my spirit, the buzz surged in me, like someone squeezing my hand. When I entered an extended time of worship, the buzz turned into the full-blown fire.

This experience with God's Spirit drastically altered my spirituality. I exude a deeper joy that many have noticed. I share the gospel with greater freedom and spiritual authority and have more compassion for the hurting. I pray and worship with a deeper awareness of God's presence, even receiving vision-like messages from God. My faith has grown. I repented of deep-seated unbelief. My expectations of God had been very low. Now he fills me so much that even an academic like me, slow to perceive things in the spiritual realm, cannot help but trust God for greater things. For the first time I see the sick healed when I minister God's love to people. I still experience discouragement and struggle to believe at times. Yet my experience of God's personal attention has given my faith a new dimension.

EMPOWERED FOR THE HURTING

This was nowhere more evident than in my efforts to minister to a woman named Vanessa. I met Señora Vanessa in 2000 when I came to Venezuela on my second visit. On our last day, she approached me with a handwritten note. She insisted that I translate it for a young Canadian man from our group named Rick. My heart sank when I realized the desperation of the scribbled message. "Please take my boy. Raise him as your own. Little Danny has no future here. Take him to your country."

As I read the letter, Rick's face flushed in disbelief. Speechless, with his heart on his sleeve, he stumbled helplessly into the conundrum. "I am . . . so sorry, Señora. But I . . . cannot take your boy." There wasn't a dry eye among us.

Seven years later a bullet to Danny's abdomen ended his short life. Barely twenty years of age, Danny fathered one child and lived a generic life of irresponsibility that included occasional street crime. Yet he never neglected his mother, whom he loved dearly.

Since moving into the slum, my family has lived a short walk from Señora Vanessa's dilapidated wooden shack. For the most part I viewed her and her family as overwhelmingly dysfunctional and impoverished, beyond my capacity to deal with. I avoided walking past her place. My faith wasn't big enough to imagine good things for her. Team members and occasional visitors exhibited more faith, visiting her, praying for her, and extending practical help.

After Danny's death and my renewal in the Holy Spirit, I stopped at Señora Vanessa's home. The trauma of Danny's death left her blind. This normally overweight woman lost over thirty pounds due to the diabetic condition she contracted a year earlier. Now despite her loss of eyesight, physically weakened body, emotionally-spent state, and the almost unbearable stench of a damp and dirty makeshift shack, I found myself strangely attracted to her home and to engaging her in conversation.

After finding the largest rock to sit on in her dirt-patch patio, I invited her into a time of healing prayer. I led her back to the pain and trauma of Danny's shooting, to the moment of her perceived abandonment by God. She openly confessed to me her rage toward God. Like the friends of the paralytic in Mark 2, I exercised the faith that Jesus had not abandoned her at that painful moment of loss, but that he was present with her. When I voiced this to her, I invited her to "see" him using her holy imagination ("Where do you see him?"). She reported seeing Jesus at her side as they loaded Danny's nearly lifeless body into the ambulance.

I pulled out my guitar and we ended our time with a song I composed for use in healing prayer ministry. We must have sung it twenty times. At one point, she yelled over to her very disinterested adolescent daughter, "Ana, come here. Learn this song so you can help me sing it in bed tonight." The verse that spoke to her heart and became her bedtime prayer reads, "I believe you, God. I trust you, Lord. I receive your Word in me. I confess to you, your right over my life."

When I returned later, I noticed a remarkable peace about her. She talked as a woman of faith. She had encountered Christ and knew it. She scolded me for my obvious surprise. "You taught me how to pray. I was so angry with God. But I repented of my rage because Jesus showed me that he was with me during the whole episode of Danny's death. I'm not angry with God anymore."

For several years I have theologized and taught from 1 John 4:19: "We love because he first loved us." As the Great Initiator, God came to us first and keeps coming first. We are the responders. Out of our experience of his love, we love and bless others. Far from being indifferent toward my theological work, God—by his Spirit—initiated once again, stepping right into my sacred thinking, enhancing it in completely unexpected ways.

8

Spiritual Power Reassessed

No one reads Scripture experience free. For integrity's sake, we must do our best to articulate our cultural assumptions and become aware of the grid we use to interpret the Bible. Problems arise when we read from our perspective without recognizing it.

Liberation theologians contributed this insight to the church's global theological conversation. They rightly insisted that every theology is the product of the context in which it's conceived. Context is never neutral or pure. European and North American theologians cannot see their work as simply "theology" while blacks do "black theology" and women do "feminist theology." Every theology carries an ideology whether acknowledged or not. And no theology exists apart from the particularities of the theologian doing it.

My encounter with the Holy Spirit dramatically impacted how I understand Scripture regarding the Spirit. I cannot pretend otherwise. In the following interpretive work I try to steer clear of two extremes: on the one hand, the pretense of interpreting Scripture from an experience-free posture; and on the other, unchecked, experience-inspired interpretations. There is tension in any attempt to balance these interpretive factors. Yet it's a balancing act that integrity requires. What follows is more theological than exegetical and more personal than systematic.

SATAN'S ROLE IN THE BIBLICAL NARRATIVE

Before my "dunking" in the Spirit, I minimized Satan's work in the world. My lack of experience with dark spirits left me with a limited understanding of the schemes of the devil. I came face-to-face with my deficiency while reviewing a teaching tool I created for house churches in the slums. The pictorial narrative of the biblical story depicted Adam and Eve with a dark, jagged line separating them. In a kind of "aha" moment, I saw my theological blind spot. There was no serpent! Someone without biblical knowledge would have come to the conclusion that the only problem posed by Scripture is human rebellion. That's not how the text reads.

"Now the serpent was more crafty than any of the wild animals the Lord God had made. He said to the woman, 'Did God really say, "You must not eat from any tree in the garden?"'" (Gen 3:1). "When the woman saw that the fruit of the tree was good for food and pleasing to the eye, and also desirable for gaining wisdom, she took some and ate it. She also gave some to her husband, who was with her, and he ate it" (Gen 3:6).

Which problem arises first in the text, human rebellion or Satan's deception? Which one leads to the other? Do humans sin and then the devil finds a foothold? The text places Satan's deception at the root of the crisis, fundamental to the human dilemma in the world God created.

I wasn't alone in neglecting the work of God's adversary. Much of the Gospel literature produced in the United States and used around the world puts the overwhelming theological weight on human sin to the great neglect of the evil one's role.

This is not an either/or situation. We can address human rebellion and our need for reconciliation with God, *and* underscore the role of Satan's deception. When we fail to see the problem of Satan, we fail to see God's victory over sin, death, *and* the devil. This results in disciples and missionaries (!) who are ill equipped to defeat the works of the evil one.

PAUL'S POSITIVITY TOWARD SPIRITUAL GIFTS (1 COR 12–14)

To defeat the works of the evil one, we need all that God has for us. Prior to my recent experiences with the Holy Spirit, I believed that:

- Paul's basic stance toward the gifts mentioned in 1 Corinthians 12 and 14 was only cautiously positive
- We shouldn't seek gifts, only the Giver
- To seek the gifts is dubious at best; at worst, it's a dangerous deviation from the singlehearted pursuit of the Giver
- If we seek the gifts, we aren't seeking love

Consider Paul in his own words from 1 Corinthians 12–14:

- 12:1: "Now about spiritual gifts, brothers, I do not want you to be ignorant."
- 12:31: "Eagerly desire the greater gifts."
- 14:1: "Follow the way of love and eagerly desire spiritual gifts, especially the gift of prophecy."
- 14:5: "I would like everyone of you to speak in tongues, but I would rather have you prophesy."
- 14:12: "Since you are eager to have spiritual gifts, try to excel in gifts that build up the church."
- 14:18: "I thank God that I speak in tongues more than all of you."
- 14:39: "Be eager to prophesy, and do not forbid speaking in tongues."

The apostle didn't pit seeking God against seeking the gifts. Paul apparently saw no contradiction in these two desires of the heart. This is remarkable when we consider the reported abuses and chaos that the Corinthian church allowed in their gatherings. In an environment that required order and correction, Paul felt strong enough about the role of spiritual gifts in the church to encourage the believers to eagerly seek "the greater gifts" and continue their practice in the congregation.

Paul wrote to address the problem of divisions in the church resulting from the believers' ignorance and misuse in the exercise of spiritual gifts. Instead of creating Christlike community and honoring everyone, the spiritual gifts divided the community, with some members esteemed over others. Paul's correction brought order to the exercise of the gifts and pointed them to love as the most excellent way.

The apostle never abandoned the gifts and their use in the church. Nor did he question the Corinthian's pursuit of God because of their eagerness to receive the Holy Spirit's gifts. His disposition towards the gifts remained positive throughout the passage.

PENTECOST AND THE GIFT OF THE HOLY SPIRIT

In my noncharismatic upbringing, phrases like "baptism of the Spirit" divided churches and closed off people like me from a deeper experience with the Holy Spirit. I never identified with such terms or the teaching associated with them. Even now, I feel more comfortable referring to my experiences with descriptive expressions that evoke curiosity rather than rejection (e.g., "when God dunked me" in the Spirit, "the Spirit fell on me," or "immersed me in the Spirit").

As a teenager I resented the implication that what I had wasn't enough. Hadn't I repented and trusted Jesus as Lord? Isn't there only one baptism? Didn't the apostle Paul get upset about preachers who required faith in Jesus plus something else?

Yet I couldn't deny that Jesus himself needed to be empowered by the Spirit before he began his public ministry. Though Jesus was the Messiah and his mission was unique, he repeatedly linked his ministry with the ministry of his followers. He gave them his authority to do his ministry. He promised to give his disciples the same Spirit with which he had been empowered. He declared that they would do "even greater" works. When he prepared his friends for his departure, he commissioned them, "As the Father sent me, so I send you."

The Acts narrative describes this "gift" (1:4), "promise" (1:4), "filling" (2:4), "baptism" (1:5), "Holy Spirit coming on you" (1:8) as being given for empowerment in witness. "You will receive power . . . and you will be my witnesses" (1:8). It's not about getting into the kingdom. It's a gift that enables fruitful ministry. If I understand witnessing to be more than just words, I'll see the Holy Spirit's empowerment as more than a preaching gift. It will include deeper matters of my person and the fruit of the Spirit while stopping short of becoming a cureall for character flaws.

HEARING THE VOICE OF GOD

More than ever I find myself in the school of prayer, learning to recognize God's voice. To speak of "hearing God's voice" can sound presumptuous. I don't "hear" God as I hear my neighbor. God's communication is different from ordinary conversation between humans. Nevertheless, God does communicate with us. To live as if he didn't would be equally presumptuous.

How does God speak to us? And, how do we "hear" him? Many noteworthy books have been written on this topic. I will only touch on the use of imagination in prayer. I do this for two reasons. First, because evangelicals have been generally skeptical of imaginative prayer, drawing a sharp line between what's considered the objective (written) word of God and subjective (intuitive) divine guidance. Secondly, since the Holy Spirit filled me, my communion with God has been greatly enhanced through the holy exercise of my imagination.

J. I. Packer, a leading spokesperson for North American evangelical thought and practice, addresses the issue of Christians using imagination in prayer in his seminal work *Knowing God*.[1] Packer is essentially negative, discouraging Christians from using their imagination in prayer. He wants to avoid breaking the second commandment, "You shall not make for yourself an idol (graven image) in the form of anything in heaven above or on the earth below or in the waters below."

Packer believes that images of Jesus in one's imagination constitute the worship of a representation of God. Representations are by nature not God, and therefore idolatrous. If such an image is not really God, it is a false god and possibly demonic. The two questions at the heart of Packer's concern are: (1) Are we making graven images through the use of imagination in prayer? and (2) are we seeing God or a false god? Packer answers the first question with a gentle yet clear "Yes." To the second question, he argues that biblically, "no one has ever seen God" (John 1:18; 1 John 4:12). To claim otherwise is to risk committing a grave sin.

Brad Jersak, a Canadian pastor, offers a different perspective on these two questions.[2] It is true, he says, that no one has ever seen God as he is with his or her natural eyes. Yet King David testified, "As for me, I shall behold your face in righteousness. I will be satisfied with your likeness when I awake" (Ps 17:15) and "I saw the Lord always before me. Because he is at my right hand, I will not be shaken" (Ps. 16:8). Some encounters in Scripture were described as "face-to-face"—Jacob's wrestling with God, Moses' encounter with God in the tent of meeting, and the children of Israel at Mount Sinai (Gen 32:30; Num 14:14; Deut 5:4). God's judgments during the time of Ezekiel were executed face-to-face (Ezek 20:35).

---

1. Packer, *Knowing God*, 50–51.
2. Jersak, *Can You Hear Me?* 91–100.

These meetings were mediated in some way. The people saw God via the angel of the Lord, in a vision, in the fire, the cloud, and so on. No one has ever seen God directly with the naked eye. Yet Scripture gives testimony that God can and should be seen with the eyes of the heart. Paul speaks of this tension in 1 Corinthians 13: "Now we see but a poor reflection as in a mirror; then we shall see face-to-face. Now I know in part; then I shall know fully, even as I am fully known."

Jersak uses the example of the sun's image as it reflects off the surface of water. Are you looking at the sun? Yes and no. Is that really the sun you're seeing? Yes and no. We know better than to look directly at the sun. Even the reflection of the sun on water blinds. Although we look at a reflected image of the sun, it's fair to say that we see the sun in the water. Thus when you "see" the Lord in a visualization prayer, do you see God? Yes and no. It's not God "as he is," but it may be a true image of the Lord revealed to you by God's Spirit.

When visualization is activated independently of a relationship with God or guided by any spirit other than the Spirit of Christ, we must beware (1 John 4:1–4). Yet the fear of many goes beyond this biblical warning. Satan's ability to place deceptive images in the mind makes it necessary for some to erect a prohibition against all visualization.

Virtually everyone has pictured Bible stories of Jesus with the use of imagination. We've watched the *Jesus* film, which conveys images of Christ according to an actor's portrayal. According to Packer's logic, these practices represent a serious danger, since viewers see an image of Jesus that's not really him. He treats imagination as an enemy to be feared, not a gift for our edification. If visual pictures in our minds have power to influence us down destructive paths, as no one disputes, shouldn't Spirit-inspired mental images lead us into deeper relationship with God? Or do we consider the mind the sole domain of the devil and our flesh?

THE HOLY SPIRIT'S WORK

According to John's Gospel, the Holy Spirit does many things. He teaches, testifies, glorifies, reveals, reminds, guides, dwells with, comforts, accompanies, and convicts. The Spirit is called the Comforter/Counselor/Advocate. Jesus sent the Holy Spirit to us from the Father. He proceeds from the Father and gives testimony to the Son. Yet he's also sent by the Father in the name of the Son. The Holy Spirit teaches us "all things," guides us to "all truth," and reminds us of Christ's teachings, speaking on the Son's behalf to reveal what's to come.

My experience forced me to reexamine how the Spirit does these things. When he fell on me the first time, God convicted me of my deep-seated unbelief. He taught me faith through his dramatic, physical flooding of my body and soul.

Physical phenomena like speaking in tongues, laughing in the Spirit, and burning hands aren't self-authenticating. They must be tested to ensure that the Spirit at work teaches, testifies, and glorifies Jesus through such manifestations. Exceptional phenomena don't constitute a deep spirituality, a reward for godly living, or a guarantee of spiritual power. I experience them as gestures of God's loving presence, a strange and wonderful grace that draws me to the Lord. They also convict me of my need for God.

In my case, the dramatic nature of the Spirit's filling hasn't been in direct proportion to the spiritual power I've experienced in ministry to others. There's no mechanical logic at work that dictates, "If you're slain in the Spirit for x number of hours or you experience y phenomenon, you'll receive z amount of anointing for ministry." I'm the first to admit, not without some frustration, that the spiritual gifting that's resulted from my rather extreme experience of the Holy Spirit has been quite ordinary. I'm human, and struggle with the tension between accepting myself "in accordance with the measure of faith God has given me" (Rom 12:3) and "eagerly desiring spiritual gifts, especially the gift of prophecy" (1 Cor 14:1).

SPIRITUAL POWER SERVES LOVE

Paul's charge to "eagerly desire spiritual gifts" comes on the coattails of the more fundamental charge to "follow the way of love." The sequence and relationship between the two are critical. They belong together—semantically in our thinking and practically in the life of the church. Paul mentions the two charges in one sentence.

The greatest commandment is to love God. The second, "that is like it," is to love one's neighbor (Matt 22:37–39). Jesus gave his disciples what he called a "new commandment . . . to love one another." By this "all people will know that you are my disciples" (John 13:34). Last but not least, Paul's manifesto of divine love in 1 Corinthians 13 places love above faith and hope: "these three remain; but the greatest of these is love."

How does spiritual power relate to love? Luke 10:20 records the return of the seventy, overjoyed with their successful mission. They exercised spiritual power and authority in healing the sick and setting people free from demons. Jesus didn't elevate their experience of power. He put it in proper relation to greater matters: "Do not rejoice that the spirits submit to you, but rejoice that your names are written in heaven."

Recently my wife, Birgit, and I sat with our friend Claudia, a resident in barrio San Pedro you'll get to know in later chapters. She shared with us how she ministered physical healing to a neighbor. I affirmed her gift of faith and the Holy Spirit's fiery presence in her burning hands, which administered God's healing. Tasting God's spiritual power operating through her clearly encouraged her. Though I wasn't wrong in affirming God's power at work in her, I could have done more to help her place the experience within the bigger picture. I confess that Luke 10:20 didn't come to mind until later.

Luke 10 shows that spiritual power is subordinate to the greater question of our belonging in God. Power and love are seamless because we belong to One who shares his power with us. As his children, we know his love and power.

Jesus himself demonstrated how spiritual power served love throughout his earthly ministry. In John 4, Jesus exercised the gift of prophecy (or a "gift of knowledge") with great attention and care to the woman and her whole community. This Gospel narrative leaves me just as impressed with the Holy Spirit's power to break down racial and religious divisions as the ability to prophetically see into a troubled woman's personal life.

Fortunately, we don't have to choose. As I describe in the next chapter, I call this the power of Acts 2 serving the paradigm of Acts 10, which is nothing less than the church ministering in both dimensions of Pentecost in one, integrated whole. For the age of the Spirit in which we live is more than the visible display of spiritual power evidenced in Acts 2—if we dare to follow the Advocate's trailblazing lead.

9

God's Spirit Crosses Lines

> I will establish` my covenant as an everlasting covenant between me and you and your descendants after you . . . and this is the covenant you are to keep: every male among you shall be circumcised. (Gen 17:7, 10)

THE HOLY SPIRIT OUTPOURING at Pentecost established the church and its subsequent expansion. Yet the birthing of the church, as recorded in Acts 2, didn't change much of the apostle Peter's thinking. He needed further revelations and conflicts to catch the bigger picture of their mission to the nations.

Peter's formation with his Master on the back roads of Palestine could have prepared him for his encounter with Cornelius in Acts 10. In John 4, Jesus concluded his extremely countercultural conversation with a Samaritan woman by accepting an invitation to stay the night in their village. In the end, Jesus and his Jewish disciples spent two nights hosted by their racial and religious adversaries. How did Peter recall the hospitality of a people no better than uncircumcised gentiles, yet whose faith in Jesus made them his brothers and sisters?

Even with the Samaritan village outreach in the background, Pentecost didn't empower Peter to go beyond Israel's ethnic borders with the Good News. Acts 2 didn't produce this paradigm shift in the apostle much less in the emerging Jerusalem church. Fortunately, the Spirit was only warming up.

The outpouring remained incomplete until God acted sovereignly through the Spirit to include the gentiles. In Acts 10 we read that a gentile God-fearer in Caesarea named Cornelius received a vision from God ("visions" promised by the prophet Joel). The same Spirit that fell on the one hundred-twenty Jews gathering in the upper room on Pentecost led Peter, reluctant and fearful, into this uncircumcised household.

If Acts 2 served as the *Jewish* Pentecost, Acts 10 became the *gentile* Pentecost, with the latter becoming Peter's begrudging conversion to God's vision of shalom—the new humanity, with Jews and gentiles made one in Christ apart from circumcision (Eph 2:15).

Even so, the gentile question remained unsettled for the early church. Jewish believers in Jerusalem likely continued expecting gentile converts to be circumcised. Not surprisingly, we find Jewish Christians zealous for the law traveling to Antioch, a gentile city with a trailblazing gentile church. They were concerned about a growing movement there with a purported disregard for circumcision. Paul cited this incident as a betrayal of the gospel (Gal 2:11–16). The circumcision group from Jerusalem didn't accept the gentile believers as their brothers and sisters in the Lord, and even drew Peter and Barnabas into their hypocrisy (2:12–13).

"Who is my brother?" "Who is my sister?" This was the question at the heart of the Antioch confrontation between Paul and Peter. Peter, voting with his retreating feet, essentially declared (under pressure), "The gentile believers are *not* my sisters and brothers unless they accept circumcision." Paul, filled with the same Spirit of Pentecost, countered, "That is a flat-out denial of God's Good News to the gentiles. You are betraying the Lord" (yet again!).

Today we don't feel the clash or identify with Peter's trepidation. Because of this, we don't recognize either how offensively the Spirit acted or how great the apostle Paul suffered because of this issue he pioneered. These incidents represented an enormous stumbling block for Peter and the Jerusalem church. Far from downplaying the apostle's difficulty, the text makes much of the scandal and what it meant for the church.

The confrontation between the apostles, cited in Paul's letter to the Galatians, must have occurred after Peter's encounter with Cornelius and before the Jerusalem council. This council, as recorded in Acts 15, took a big step forward by recognizing gentile believers as brothers and sisters apart from circumcision while urging them to avoid "food sacrificed to idols."

Indicative of the ongoing ambiguity surrounding the issue, we find Paul going even further in his letter to the Romans by declaring all foods clean. This gave gentile believers there the freedom to eat such foods within the guidelines of love and respect for a church of diverse convictions (Rom 14:14). It would be an understatement to say that unanimity was lacking on this point.

According to the Acts of the Apostles, any hopes we have of a one-off Holy Spirit outpouring (quick fix) to solve all our interpersonal, interracial, inter-ecclesial challenges goes out the window. Even with Acts 2's spiritual power released for Acts 10 ministries of line-crossing, the testimony of Scripture squeezes yet more patience out of us. The power of Acts 2, and the courageous line-crossing of Acts 10, still requires trial and error in the ongoing give and take of Christian community and mission. Though perhaps sobering to our typically glossy view of the "New Testament" church, the Spirit-filled early church processed these deep, paradigmatic changes through many fits and starts.

REREADING GALATIANS

We typically read Galatians as a rebuttal to legalism. We believe Paul unleashed his fury against Christians teaching a message of Jesus plus human effort, salvation by faith *and* works. Yet the "works of the law" that concern the apostle are repeatedly cited as circumcision and, by implication, other Jewish practices (such as food laws and Sabbath keeping). At issue here is not human effort per se but the works found in the Torah (the Jewish Law). Paul is irate at Jewish Christians for drawing a Jesus-plus-circumcision line between themselves and gentile believers.

The matter in question was, who belongs to God's family? Jewish Christians answered unequivocally that gentile believers don't belong unless they become like us, since God's covenant came to us and circumcision is an everlasting sign of that covenant.

Paul cried from the depths of his soul, No! Jesus' cross set us free from these works of the Law. Gentile believers belong to God's one people apart from circumcision. What matters is not whether we are circumcised. What matters is belonging to God's new creation in Christ (Gal 4:26; 6:15).

This reading has the power to offend us today. No longer can we safely identify with Paul (against that cowardly, compromising Peter) by virtue of our ability to cultivate a spirituality free of legalism (a lifelong process with more than enough pitfalls). We are confronted by our "Judaizing" views and Peter-like actions toward brothers and sisters in

Christ's body that we avoid at all costs and treat as non-family. (Unless, of course, they become like us!)

TORONTO, HOLDEN, & CT

After the Holy Spirit fell on me, I encountered "gentile believers" whose faith wasn't like mine. My new friend, Bob Ekblad, invited me to join him at a pastors' conference in Toronto. I was shocked. Toronto? Those are the crazy, "lion-roaring" extremists that made such a splash in the mid-'90s. They couldn't still be around! To me, they didn't exist. According to my attitude and actions, they didn't belong to the church. They weren't my brothers and sisters. I'd heeded the clear message from the guardians of evangelical orthodoxy: "Stay away from them. They're dangerous." I felt justified in ignoring them.

I knew the charismatic movement from my experience with the Vineyard church and the ministry of John Wimber. Yet the Toronto folks were an altogether different crowd, completely new to me. Toronto was and still is a revival center. Imagine charismatics with the heat turned up a few notches.

To my surprise, the conference was the happiest week of my life, or so I described it to friends afterward. The joy and exuberance flowed in rivers. Imagine a thousand pastors behaving like carefree children—loved and free, running and jumping in abandonment, overwhelmed by their heavenly father's pleasure. One big joy fest! Though I didn't completely identify with my revivalist brothers and sisters, I discovered that they were just that: my family—with much to teach me!

The following year I took a sabbatical rest in the United States. I stayed at a beautiful, remote mountain community of the Evangelical Lutheran Church of America (ELCA) called Holden Village. For those familiar with mainline denominations, the ELCA touts their inclusiveness and tolerance of diversity. They ordain practicing gays and lesbians and exude an admirable spirituality of mystery, creativity, and beauty.

My time at Holden was remarkably similar to the Toronto conference. (What?) Though in many ways I didn't identify with my mainline brothers and sisters, I experienced them as my Christian family with much to teach me.

Holden Village is the most remotely inhabited locale in the forty-eight contiguous States, or so they tell me. Upon return to civilization,

I reentered the land of evangelical orthodoxy. This was best symbolized by a copy of the magazine *Christianity Today* ("CT") that I picked up somewhere. One article scathingly critiqued the Pentecostal movement in Latin America, pronouncing it heretically out of step with historic Protestantism. Another journalist unapologetically shamed an author whose views the reporter considered far enough "left" to no longer belong to the evangelical (Christian?) fold.

Who is my brother? Who is my sister? This question clearly didn't die with the apostles.

FOLLOWING THE SPIRIT TO CORNELIUS

When I first visited Caracas in 1998, I brought a team composed of evangelicals and Catholics. We were invited to survey the slums and discern whether to launch an InnerCHANGE work. Since the early '90s when one of our missionaries converted to Roman Catholicism, an InnerCHANGE has bridged the Catholic/Protestant divide. Though the team we eventually deployed to Venezuela in 2001 consisted of only evangelicals, we made an effort from the beginning to work with the local Catholic parish as well as a Methodist-Pentecostal congregation.

As a team we navigate these waters with great care. We learned on our survey trip that if evangelicals experience Catholics for the ministers they are before knowing their church affiliation, they get "cornered" by God's Spirit into accepting them. As one Venezuelan Baptist put it after ministering with our team in the jail and discovering that some were Catholic, "I don't care what church you're from. If you come back, my door will always be open."

Recently, we've seen the Holy Spirit taking the lead in bridging this divide beyond our direct efforts. One of the youth leaders in the local parish, whom I'll call Jaime, is a classmate of the Methodist pastor's son, Carlos. Jaime and Carlos are, in fact, quite good friends. Through their friendship, five of the Catholic youth joined the evangelical youth on a Methodist youth retreat.

The next Sunday, two InnerCHANGE team members and my son, John Mark, went to 9:00 a.m. mass. Jaime and his friends, obviously animated from the retreat, then walked with the three evangelical visitors to the 11:00 a.m. Methodist service. Afterward, the Catholics invited the evangelicals to play soccer back at the Catholic church. The Methodist youth knew they needed permission. The pastor permitted them to go "for one hour." (In other words, "Leave as soon as you can!")

The next week I began a twelve-week hermeneutics class at the Methodist church. Lo and behold, Jaime walked in with four of his Catholic comrades in tow. One highlight from the richness of the joint learning experience was our treatment of Paul's Letter to the Galatians. We put together a skit to dramatize the conflict that the apostle cites in chapter 2. Under pressure from Jewish Christians, Peter retreated from sharing table fellowship with uncircumcised believers. Jaime and another Catholic played the role of the gentile Christians, the obvious outsiders, with the evangelicals playing that of the Jewish Christians.

The topic came to a head when the ancient issue took on contemporary flesh and bones—and names! Paul insisted that Jews could be family with uncircumcised believers, that the "Israel of God" (Gal 6:16) didn't require non-Jewish people to become Jewish. Sitting there among believers from both sides of the contemporary ecclesial divide, I asked the evangelicals if Catholics have to become evangelical to be saved and belong to God's family. The more immediate questions was, were Jaime and his friends our brothers and sisters in the Lord, or did they have to become like us?

The lesson ended as inconclusively as the prodigal parable, where the elder son remained outside the party. Yet the story continues. Shortly after my course, a mixed (or should I say "united") team of InnerCHANGE missionaries visited us. With the Methodist pastor and several of his elders at his side, my friend Nate Bacon, a Catholic InnerCHANGE missionary, gave a talk on Christian unity in the Methodist church.

As I write, five months have passed since this process began, and just last week twenty youth (!) from the Catholic parish attended the small Methodist all-church annual retreat.

The Holy Spirit is taking the lead, going places that will certainly challenge and stretch his people. This shouldn't sur-

> prise us since Jesus expected his Good News to be offensive; he called those who were not scandalized by his line-crossing mission "blessed" (Matt 11:6).

OFFENSIVE LINE CROSSING TODAY

The Holy Spirit took Peter across a line—a line created by religion, yet ironically one that religion-inspired mission must violate if we are to be true to God's intentions and the actions of the Holy Spirit. In InnerCHANGE, we consider this the prophetic dimension of our ministry—the difficult task of revealing with our hands and feet (and mouths) a "fault line" in the church, a debilitating blind spot. This is usually not without controversy.

This is prophetic in the biblical sense. Like the prophets of old, we call the church back to its biblical foundation as image bearers of our Creator God with love for God and neighbor, especially the least and last—even when such actions appear to many as "anti-American." (Have you loved a terrorist lately? How about a communist?)

In cross-cultural work this means I must resist the "Judaizing" temptation to teach Jesus plus American democracy, Jesus plus anti-communism, Jesus plus evangelical church membership, or any other equivalent to Jewish circumcision as the absolute rite of belonging, even when such a position is expected and applauded by my evangelical donor constituency. I must join Peter in Cornelius' house even when "James' group" (Gal 2:12) at headquarters could fire me. This implies the humility to enter new and different cultures as a listener and learner without a role that allows me to control the way emerging national leaders express the gospel.

On the American homefront, this line-crossing mission means that "Toronto" needs "Holden," who in turn needs "CT." We the church need the whole Acts of the Apostles—the spiritual power of Acts 2, dramatically expressed by today's revivalist leaders, *and* the paradigm-challenging power of Acts 10 (and Acts 15). This is displayed by courageous leaders like my friend Bob Ekblad, who dares to forge relationships of mutuality with leaders from all three camps.

The Spirit of Pentecost that brought together Peter and Cornelius says to us, "Love those you disagree with. Get to know them as the brothers and sisters they are. You need each other *because* of your differences." Wouldn't the apostle to the gentiles have argued that Jewish believers needed to learn from gentile believers?

Many years ago a dear friend "came out of the closet." Susan, as I'll call her, was an evangelist and church planter par excellence. As a practicing homosexual she continued serving the Lord in a church that encouraged the gay lifestyle. Whenever we met, Susan used the full extent of her persuasion skills to convince me of the biblical basis for her new life.

After several visits I realized that Susan couldn't accept me unless I agreed with her. Every conversation ended in marked discord. I earnestly pleaded with her to stop trying to change me in hopes that we could salvage some degree of friendship. She couldn't let me be, and we both lost a dear friend.

In the language of 1 Corinthians 12, Christian family, defined as communion with those I uniformly agree with, is no longer a body with its diverse parts. It becomes instead a deformed mutation that grossly misrepresents the intentions of its Creator. True body life means remaining family while retaining differences—loving without agreeing, holding diverse convictions while genuinely engaging the other.

In InnerCHANGE, we live this day in and day out between Catholic and Protestant members of our mission community. Though we hold to essential, historic tenets of biblical Christianity, we don't agree on many finer details of doctrine and practice. Nor do we have to in order to live and work as a missionary, prophetic, and contemplative Christian order among the poor. Within these three "currents" with which we describe our vocation, we find ample room to walk together, even with our differences. With Jesus leading and the poor as companions on the road, our disagreements lose their weightiness.

This is a lesson the early church struggled to practice and a paradigm the apostle Paul taught in Romans 14. Some first-century Christians believed that eating food sold in the market that had been sacrificed to pagan idols violated God's eternal law. To dine on such foods, for them, was ethically wrong and spiritually harmful. Paul disagreed and proposed guidelines for believers of diverse convictions to belong together in one church community.

Today we also disagree in the church regarding what constitutes a violation of God's true way. Pick the issue. That which is negotiable to one is nonnegotiable to another, be it practicing gays, prosperity preachers, or, I would add, American Christians going to war and shedding their blood out of allegiance to their nation (which I believe to be idolatrous). We don't agree on many issues. Yet we're brothers and sisters in Christ.

One argument I've heard from the "CT" segment of the church is that if evangelicals enlarge the circle of fellowship to include "Holden" or "Toronto," even while respecting each other's differences, such "table-sharing" will confuse the weaker members of Christ's body, causing them to stumble. Paul's advice in Romans 14 addresses this explicitly and implicitly.

Explicitly, he instructs believers who disagree over ethics to "make every effort to do what leads to peace and to mutual edification" (14:19). He implores both sides to sacrifice for the sake of the other. They are to curb their behavior in each other's presence to not "destroy God's work" (v. 20) or "destroy your brother for whom Christ died" (v. 15), and to "keep what you believe between yourself and God" (v. 22). This last piece of advice is something I practice regularly as I walk among "liberals" one day and "conservatives" the next.

Implicitly, Paul expected the church to overcome the absolutizing ways of religion, which in the end are worldly and anti-gospel. God's Spirit, like Christ our Savior, is non-absolutizing. Even if I'm right (and God agrees with me!), God won't champion my cause, in my way, to vindicate me and castigate my adversary!

We all believe that we hold to truthful doctrinal and theological positions. No one serves God and the church while dispassionately considering their beliefs up for grabs to the highest bidder. I fervently hold my convictions of what I believe to be right. I must also be humble enough to affirm that though I might be correct in one position, I will most certainly in wrong in another. No one scores 100 percent on the truth scale, if there were such a thing. No one can honestly lay claim to complete understanding and rightness in all matters of doctrine and practice. We're a body. We need each other. We're incomplete when left to ourselves.

The Spirit that flowed at Pentecost empowered the church to reach the nations and leads us today across absolutized lines into God's irresistible shalom. This affirmation is all too true when we consider the historical and sociopolitical context of Caracas' violent slums and the courageous, pioneering, Paul-like leaders needed to broker God's peace fest.

10

God's Spirit Incarnates

On July 25, 1567, Don Diego Losada founded the town that became Caracas. Within a short time, Losada and his fellow Spaniards committed three acts of great historical significance. First, upon arrival at the port of La Guaira, which leads to the valleys of the present-day capital, he declared, "I take possession of these lands in the name of God and the king." Second, he and the founders began the bloody extermination of the indigenous tribes that occupied these valleys. Third, they built—for the glory of God and the king—the Church of St. Francis, which stands today in the historic center of Caracas.[1]

To do justice to the historical picture of the sixteenth-century conquistadores, we must acknowledge that the strong, conquering Christ brought to the New World constitutes only half of the conquest's story. The other half of this tragic episode in church history is that of the suffering Savior—typically portrayed as the baby Jesus in the loving arms of his mother Mary, and as the bleeding, agonizing Redeemer on the cross. In the name of this God—both terrible and tender—the Spaniards subjugated tribe after tribe, simultaneously massacring and "Christianizing" the peoples.

---

1. Delgado, *Caracas*, 61.

Church of St. Francis, built by the early conquistadores in the heart of Caracas, and still a place of worship today

The Pentecostal movement that swept through Latin America in the last century can also be viewed through these historical juxtapositions. Not unlike their Spanish forefathers, they have largely opted for a victorious, healing Christ and a spirituality that they themselves describe as *de conquista* (a "conquering" way). With the expansive growth of Pentecostalism in the region, they'll likely seize increasing political power and exercise it forcefully.

In a context characterized by such paradigmatic extremes, we've felt compelled to teach the mystery of the incarnation—the *one* Christ who combines in a mysterious and upside-down way both majesty *and* humility, power *and* weakness. This is the Deliverer whose birth—both powerful and humble in nature—was announced to the shepherds: "Today in the town of David, a Savior is born. He is the Messiah, the Lord. This will be a sign to you: You will find a baby wrapped in clothes and lying in a manger" (Luke 2:11–12).

The biblical snapshot of the Lord of Lords in the vulnerability of a newborn baby is more than an impressive reminder of the lengths to which God went to enter our world. This picture also serves as a controlling paradigm that gets replayed throughout the Gospel narratives. We see this in the thirsty Messiah asking the Samaritan woman for water at the well, in the humble carpenter-turned-rabbi calming the raging sea with a word, and in the promised king entering Jerusalem on a donkey. Finally, we witness this in the One with power to save others while refusing to save himself, only to be vindicated on the third day. As a community of missionaries, our presence in the slums puts flesh and bones to this mystery.

LIVING THE MYSTERY WITH CATHOLICS

Father Enrique, the local priest in our slum, invited me to join him for a meeting with the leaders of two grassroots Christian communities. Enrique picked me up in his rather run-down Jeep. We made the short drive up the hillside and pulled into a narrow alleyway that appeared out of nowhere. Friendly waves and *gritos* ("yells") welcomed us. With help from some young men, Enrique managed to squeeze his car enough to one side of the path to allow pedestrians to pass.

The meeting was intended to restart two of the parish's neighborhood Bible groups. For most of the reunion I sat at Enrique's side, watching him do his work. I didn't know what to expect, though I knew he trusted me enough that he wanted his people to know me.

When the group expressed their desire to make home visits, Enrique invited me to speak. "Brother John and his team have experience doing that." I didn't know what I would say until the words came out of my mouth. "In our experience of visiting homes, we encounter many people with evil spirits." Every head nodded. They too knew about demons.

The following week, teammate Katie McClure and I met with one of the groups. The leader, an elderly woman named Silvia, had invited us. The meeting was small and personal. Because of what I shared in the large gathering with the priest, she said to me in front of her group, "Every time I close my eyes to pray, an evil spirit manifests and stops me. Will you pray for me?"

A few days later Silvia and her daughter Sonia came over for prayer. Sonia complained of a painful ache in both arms from her neck to her hands. For three months she experienced no relief from the pain. She consumed pain pills like candy. As we prayed, I saw in my spirit that Jesus stood behind her. With loving arms he touched each shoulder at the place of her affliction. When I spoke this out to her, she jumped up from her chair and turned to me with a glowing smile on her face. "That's exactly what he's doing!" Not only did Sonia's pain disappear, but God also doused her in his love!

We also led Silvia through a thorough inventory of demonic spiritual allegiances that she had practiced over the years. God gave her the grace to repent of and renounce each one. She experienced a deep and lasting freedom to pray and worship God unencumbered by evil emissaries. Before leaving, Sonia said to her mother, "Thanks to this experience with brother John and Katie, if any more evil spirits bother you, we can take care of them ourselves. We know how to pray."

Later, Silvia and Sonia came by to catch up after I got back from a trip. From the day we prayed for Sonia's healing, she hasn't taken another pain pill. The aching never came back. Then Sonia stepped out and prayed for her husband's severe intestinal problem. God healed him. She had a similar experience of praying for another sick man from her family. God healed him too. They testified about a bad spirit in her mother's house that robbed the place of peace for many years. Following our example, she prayed with Christ's authority, sending the spirit away. The house is now full of God's peace, a dramatic transformation in the spiritual climate of the property. Two of the men in their household stopped drinking and began contributing financially to the family's needs.

This is a sign of the *one* Christ—both strong and weak, revealed in the humility of a leader like Silvia and in God's power to heal and deliver.

LIVING THE MYSTERY WITH PENTECOSTALS

For three years my wife, Birgit, and Lila Blanchard, an InnerCHANGE teammate, led a team of local Pentecostals every Monday on an outreach into barrio San Pedro (see chapter 12). San Pedro residents have seen many well-meaning Pentecostals blow through their slum with evangelistic campaigns. These ministers knock on doors, hold open-air meetings, and then exit. When Birgit and her teammate began visiting the neighborhood like clockwork every Monday with the team of volunteers from a local (non-barrio) church, the residents watched the group closely. The volunteers spent time with kids. They listened and asked questions. They joined the residents on garbage cleanup day.

The pastor had given us leadership of the volunteer outreach. This allowed us to shape the development of the ministry. Yet his people didn't know what to do with our approach. Evangelicals entering a slum with open ears and minds was unheard of. They'd been taught to preach *at* people and to remain socially distant from unbelievers. Our first job with the volunteers was to move beyond the conflictive scenario that pit our "gringo" ideas against their Venezuelan ideas. We determined to look as clearly as possible at Jesus, who we suggested would be our model for how to approach the people of the barrio. We began each Monday outreach with an open reflection on Jesus and his approach with people. The Scripture sharing went something like this:

> As Gloria is reading the passage slowly and meditatively, I want everyone to listen quietly. Do your best to enter into the story. Close your eyes and imagine the scene as it's read. This is a story of Jesus' encounter with a woman who was an outsider to Israel and even to her own village (John 4). Imagine yourself there with Jesus and the woman. After a pause for silent meditation, Gloria will read the passage a second time. Then we'll have a time to share.

What did you feel as Gloria read the story? Did you identify with anything?

I felt the woman's fear and apprehension. She didn't know what to expect from Jesus, a complete stranger to her.

Did anything strike you from the story?

I was amazed at the presence of Jesus. *[What do you mean?]* He was strong yet gentle.

What did you notice about Jesus?

His first words were to ask for water. *[Why is that important?]* Because he had a genuine need and he expressed it.

What does this teach us about God?

God is very personal. He gets down where the people are. God entrusts his message to people like the Samaritan woman.

What does this teach us about approaching people with the gospel?

Maybe we should have conversations with people. Maybe before we challenge people with their need for Jesus, we need to gain their trust. We can believe that unlikely people have great potential in the hands of God.

The residents of San Pedro kept watching . . . every Monday. What did they witness? After six months, a woman named Claudia stepped forward with the words: "I want to be like you guys!" What did Claudia see? Perhaps she detected a sign of the *one* Christ, both humble and mighty, revealed in outsiders strong enough to venture into an infamously dangerous slum and humble enough to listen and learn.

THE MYSTERY'S POWER

In Latin America, with its history of *conquistadores* who used power to exploit in the name of God and *conquistados* who were victimized and "Christianized," the incarnation speaks with special poignancy about the exercise of power. In this mystery, at the foot of the manger, we encounter an altogether different kind of might.

For those coming out of victimization and poverty, where the powerful gospel of the Spirit is all-important, the stumbling block of the incarnation is its call to vulnerability. This was evident when the local volunteers joined us in San Pedro. Assuming the posture of a listener and a learner with unbelievers was perceived as slipping into "old ways" of passivity and fatalism, even unbelief. The gospel that the Pentecostals received in Venezuela gives them the right to impose the message of Christ upon sinners. Much of their personal (or not so personal!) evangelism reflects this dynamic.

If it weren't for the witness of Scripture, strength and vulnerability might appear to be mutually exclusive. Linked as they are by God incarnate, they point unequivocally to the way we "do justice" and "love mercy" (Mic 6:8). This begs for a story.

I jogged with a man from our barrio who unknowingly led me to the manger of the child-king wrapped in swaddling clothes. Daniel was over forty years of age at the time and had recently run a 2:40 marathon. He invited me to join him at 5:30 a.m. for an eight-mile run, his daily loop.

As it turned out, Daniel just wanted to talk. When we hit the flats at the bottom of the hill, he jumped right in. "What do you think of our president?" The question caught me off guard. I made a few safe, positive remarks while confessing that I don't get caught up in the personality cult that follows him. As we ran through the streets, oblivious to the physical exertion, Daniel shared his ideals with me. I'll never forget his words.

"I want to see *your* president be the first to step forward and eliminate his own weapons of mass destruction. . . . As long as injustices like Saddam Hussein's get treated by further injustices, like those committed by your president in Iraq, we will have a world of injustices. Those in power, who could do justice, have no incentive to do what's right, since they see that solving problems with injustice gets rewarded."

Daniel sees what many of us don't. He understands that an unjust world needs its most powerful leader to give up his military strength. Daniel's vision mirrors the incarnation—a contemporary projection of the manger scene.

In Venezuelan politics, secularists and Marxists hijack this gospel portrait that Daniel paints on the canvas of international affairs. For those with political ends, this geopolitical vision makes great marketing material. It's a cause worthy of people's allegiance. Yet notice what happens. A vision of high moral character—taken from the very nature of the gospel—captivates people's loyalties. Those with power then use this vote of confidence to draw a battle line between those with the right and the wrong cause. In this scenario, conscientious Venezuelan Christians get pushed into a corner. Do they support a political ideal that resonates with the gospel, even when those championing it violate it by suppressing opposition to the cause?

U.S. politicians and pundits do the same, with a unique twist. The history of the United States, as an image of godly men and women seeking religious freedom, inspires many American Christians to pledge allegiance to the nation that shines as a "city on a hill." This vision of America as a "Christian nation" endowed by the Almighty with a special destiny makes great marketing material for plenty a mover and shaker. Unlike the WMD-divesting–world leader vision, the "benevolent" military–super-state vision looks more Constantinian than Christian. American Christians write off Daniel's idealism as nonsense. In the real world, they say, the United States is the most neighbor-friendly superpower the world is going to get. (Better America than China, they say.)

Others like myself beg to differ. If we insist on America's "Christian" founding and mission, then it doesn't suffice to compare our use of power with that of other states (be it the nineteenth-century British empire or twenty-first-century China). We must hold it up to the light of the gospel. How does our exercise of power compare to that of God in Christ? To claim we do God's bidding without holding ourselves accountable to God's ways makes us hypocritical to the world and idolatrous before the God we profess. The fact that no one expects a nation-state to behave as Christ did should be enough to give us pause.

How then do Christians, Americans and Venezuelans alike, engage politically in the vulnerability of the incarnation? There is a Christian way forward, a Jesus way of doing justice, though it's not easy.

Jesus didn't satisfy Israel or Rome. He didn't allow his movement to be hijacked or corrupted by causes of his day, traditionally sound and religiously compelling as they might have been. Rome was a snake, even if they considered themselves a benevolent power stewarding "pax romana" for the common good. Even so, Jesus didn't give his nation the right to take on Rome with military force. Nor did Jesus remain passive or indifferent. His answer was grace and judgment for everyone. In the cross, Israel and Rome faced a level playing field. Jew and gentile alike were ignorant and lost, all exposed in their rebellion. All too were recipients of mercy, unmerited and abundant.

Like Jesus, we refuse to absolutize the cause of our respective governments. By relativizing two warring sides, we don't satisfy either. Both sides consider us traitors, since they require an allegiance we can't give. Each insists on the rightness and worthiness of their position and defines patriotism as defending its actions, however mistaken they might be. Engaging both from a position of questionable loyalty is unacceptable in Washington and Caracas.

By refusing these either/or options, we love mercy and do justice Jesus style. We demonstrate a relationship to God and neighbor that embodies the DNA of God's shalom. We heed the father's invitation to join the party in mirror reflection of God's peacemaking character. Such action becomes the seedbed of God's new humanity, the hope of the nations.

Nobody likes to be seen in "Cornelius' house." No one wants to be shunned by loved ones. Yet everyone—rich and poor, male and female, slave and free, Venezuela and American—has an adversary with whom our Savior stands, to whom the Holy Spirit leads us, even as he led Peter to an "unclean" gentile family. "Stumbling" doesn't belong only to the rich (or white males!). At the cross, all stand guilty and forgiven, and challenged to reconcile through acts of mercy and justice with "this . . . our brother (or sister)."

Sooner or later each of us faces circumstances where we resist the vulnerability required of Jesus-style justice and mercy. We glory in the Almighty God who came in the humility of a manger, then drag our feet when called on to step out in the same spirit of powerlessness.

11

God's Spirit Works Paradoxically

Hopes and expectations. Though not the same, they belong together, feeding off each other. Hope is a biblical term. Expectations smacks of modern psychology and communication theory. People have expectations of each other as friends, lovers, siblings, even enemies. With God we have expectations *of* as well as hope *in*. "Hope in" leads to theological terrain. "Expectations of" invokes the immediacy of pastoral faith concerns, especially when dealing with those we have of God and ourselves. Often my expectations of God surface as a distorted hope that sabotages my service for the Lord.

As a young missionary living in the inner city of Los Angeles, California, I got blindsided by a deeply personal faith crisis. I was angry with God and out of touch with my unspoken expectations of him. In my youthful zeal I cultivated an unrealistic idealism, even conditions, of what I thought God should do through my sacrificial service. When God didn't come through according to my expectations, I hit a wall of depression that cried out, "Where's my payback, God? I'm doing my part. Now do yours!"

This isn't the only distorted hope that I wrestle with.

"POSTER CHILD" HOPE

Recently, a local couple with great promise suddenly retreated from the house church we're forming in the slums. Did they feel pressure from my expectations of them to lead? I don't know. They aren't open with me at the moment. In difficult ministries like this it's easy to place hopes (quickly and strongly) on rising stars.

In another case, Angel, a nineteen-year-old young man God saved from a street life in the gangs, oozed promise—a shining witness God was using to rescue others from the streets! Hopes grew around this dream-come-true emerging leader. Before Angel got out of the starting blocks, bullets from a passing car cut him down as he evangelized his gang friends on a street corner.

RESULTS-BASED HOPE

I also struggle with hope rooted in desired results. Though similar to the poster-child hope, this complex is different. I encountered this enemy of genuine hope when I could no longer ignore my lack of compassion for the homeless in my neighborhood. My compassionless actions toward those I considered difficult to reach were the consequence of my need to see results to sustain hope. The homeless represented a bottomless pit requiring endless efforts with little to show for it.

As a society, America proudly lays claim to much discovery and innovation. We have a deeply-embedded, can-do attitude toward life, and we bring this positivity into discipleship. To view Christian hope as less than goals reached and visions accomplished smacks of irresponsibility.

In contrast to our can-do discipleship, the apostle Paul rather pessimistically predicted to the elders of Ephesus, in whom he had invested his heart and soul, "I know that after I leave, savage wolves will come in among you and not spare the flock" (Acts 20:29). Paul expected the congregation he planted to go belly up. He didn't place his hope in the success of the churches he established.

I discover compassion for the homeless when I become conscious that what matters before God is *my* obedience, not the obedience of those I reach out to. I find refuge for this in Paul's discourse to the Ephesian elders in Acts 20:18: "You know how I lived the whole time I was with you, from the first day I came into the province of Asia. I served the Lord with great humility and with tears, although I was severely tested by the plots of the Jews."

In this stirring passage, Paul recounts his faithfulness in the ministry God entrusted to him. He underscores the difference between his obedience and the obedience of those who followed him. The former was within his control and personal responsibility. The latter wasn't.

According to the passage, Paul considered the following actions within his realm of responsibility before God:

- He served them in humility (v. 19).
- He called Jews and gentiles to repentance and faith in Jesus (v. 21).
- He taught them the whole counsel of God (v. 27).
- He never stopped warning them night and day with tears—for three years (v. 31)!
- He committed them to God and the message of God's grace (v. 32).
- He did not covet anyone's silver or gold or clothing (v. 33).
- He supplied his own material needs with his own tentmaking (v. 34).
- He modeled that the strong must help the weak (v. 35).

Paul's line of thinking also arms us to face the challenge of the gospel's offense. Faced with the incomprehensible mandate to eat what the Torah forbade, Peter followed the Holy Spirit's lead, knowing the potential ministry fallout. His obedience could cost him a "successful" pastorate in Jerusalem. So great was Peter's fear that on a later trip to Antioch, Paul rebuked him for shunning his gentile brothers and sisters when Jewish Christians arrived on the scene. Paul passionately reminded the Ephesians, as he reminded Peter in Antioch, that the heart of the matter is our faithfulness to the gospel, even when our obedience causes others to stumble and disobey.

BLAME-THE-CONTEXT HOPE

Another twisted form of hope that traps me is what I call scapegoating. According to this complex, the fault for not seeing change goes to the harsh, unforgiving environment. The context itself absorbs my disappointments. Ministering amid poverty is convenient from this standpoint. Whatever happens, or doesn't, I have an escape clause. "It's the context, what can I expect?" I keep believing in God's ultimate restoration of all things in the face of such blatant evil by taking refuge in the "badness" of the place where I serve. This is a coping strategy that accepts lack of fruit and sustains a distorted hope. Genuine hope must see the challenge of poor, urban environments differently.

MAKING SENSE OF THIS

Believing God for results in poor barrios while at the same time seeking freedom from a results-based hope might seem contradictory. Can we have it both ways? Can we experience hope that doesn't rest on results while believing the Lord for outcomes? The answer isn't a matter of simply avoiding distortions, if that were possible. Tensions and paradoxes abound, and they must make their home in us.

This reality became acute to me when in the same week I experienced the Holy Spirit's power fall on me and also our neighbors' violent murder of Caligallo. My faith in God's power to intervene in this world's affairs soared higher than ever when the Spirit's fire consumed my physical body. Then, in an equally larger-than-life moment, my despair in the face of evil's power and the absense of God's intervention dipped to new depths with the stabbing death of our friend.

God's promised new creation—in concrete, this-worldly fruit, I believe—will be born out of anointing and affliction, wonders and weakness. Hope demands that we see God's power to heal and restore in triumph *and* tragedy. This crazy hope somehow knows and believes that God's kingdom will come even when "tender shoots" like Caligallo—delivered from evil one day and chopped down by it the next—don't get a chance to take root and grow.

In this hope-filled, hope-challenged scenario, Jesus stands at the cliff's edge, and Peter stands in Cornelius' house. The Lord sets people free while suffering an obstinate people (Luke 4). The early church leader, amid prophesies and divine visions, puts his apostolic reputation on the line for the uncircumcised—a sure recipe for ecclesiastical disaster and heartache (Acts 10).

Both realities point to God's power to save and heal what is wrong in this world. Held together, we behold once again the mystery of God and his incarnation. In this tension we begin to make sense out of our hopes and expectations of God. In this paradox, we glimpse the radical middle ground we can occupy that refuses to absolutize either dimension, as if God only redeems and restores through powerful signs or unfulfilled hopes. Spiritual power and suffering—in our hands and hearts, in the human soul and the city streets—is captured uniquely in Christ, who in life and death knew God's intervening power and the lack thereof.

As I write this, we are burying a neighbor who died this week. Alexander was eighteen years old, the eldest of four brothers, all of whom suffer from muscular dystrophy. Though family, friends, and neighbors all knew his days were limited, his passing hit hard. Accompanying his younger brothers to the grave site and seeing their pain, I wondered in prayer, *God, does this have to be the future for them too? Are their premature deaths simply inevitable, to be accepted as part of this fallen world? Or is there a healing/deliverance that you'd have me pursue with the family? How do I teach Alexander's family a hope that experiences God's power making things new in the present and believes in spite of the evil one's leverage to rob and destroy?*

Part 3
Partners Outside the Gate

12

What Is a Kid to Do?

THERE WAS A KNOCK at the door. We'd moved to Venezuela only three months earlier. We lived in one of countless concrete buildings at the foot of the hillside slums while looking for a home on the hill. We were slowly getting to know people, but very few knew where we were staying. Who could it be?

When my wife, Birgit, opened the door, three children stood there looking notably forlorn. She invited them in, learned their names, and asked what they were up to. They were going door to door asking for food and water. Barbara was thirteen, Rafael nine, and Jimmy eight.

They came from a slum called San Pedro. The name was already familiar. Even as newcomers, we knew of the barrio. Its reputation for crime and violence exceeded the facts on the ground. Though small in size, San Pedro is a symbol. To the people of southwest Caracas it represents everything that is wrong about the barrios. It's also quite isolated from other slums and difficult to gain entrance.

Shortly after the encounter with the children, Birgit and I ran into them again. This time they led us to their home where Barbara introduced us to her much older half-sister Claudia.

Within months, Birgit and InnerCHANGE teammate Lila Blanchard, with a team of volunteers from the Methodist-Pentecostal Church, began a weekly climb up into San Pedro to visit and pray for families. The pastor had a burden for the children and recruited us to work there. He wanted to establish a community center in the neighborhood. He gladly delegated to InnerCHANGE the responsibility of leading the church's volunteers in this effort.

Claudia watched the volunteers faithfully climbing her hill each week. One day she surprised the group by declaring, "I want to be like you!"

NOVEMBER 29, 2005

This date is graffiti painted on a wall next to Claudia and her husband Miguel's house. Jimmy, the youngest of the three who introduced us to San Pedro with a knock on the door, was shot to death at the tender age of twelve. He was messing around with his friends. They had a gun. Oh, the things these boys do to fill their empty, aimless days! Amid their laughter and joking, one of them pulled the trigger, sending a bullet into Jimmy. He never recovered, dying before reaching the hospital. The fateful date of Jimmy's passing remains crudely sketched on the wall as a public memorial to his short-lived life.

Jimmy's mother is Hilda. Hilda and Barbara are related to Claudia through Claudia's stepmother. Jimmy grew up with six aunts and uncles living no more than one-hundred yards from his front door. These authority figures use their family roles to wreak havoc on those around them through destructive addictions to alcohol, drugs, and sexual perversions. They actively operate in the world of witchcraft and spiritism, giving themselves over to ruinous spirits. I've personally encountered two of his aunts in demonized states. What's a kid to do?

WHAT KIDS, IN FACT, DO

The first option for many is to escape. *Hit the road!* If your home life is beyond miserable . . . go to the streets! If your enemies in a small, close-knit community have put a price on your head . . . flee! Go somewhere safe. If you become a Christian, take your faith and find a safe church on the other side of town. Don't engage. It's too risky—the dangers are too great.

Taking up arms is another response to the crisis. The law of the jungle. The survival of the fittest. *Overpower your enemy!* If a cease-fire is not possible, much less genuine peace, then make sure you're in control. Ensure you have the firepower to stay on top.

WHAT SOME FAMILIES DO

Juan Carlos is a Christian from barrio San Pedro. On a visit to his home, he took me to the rooftop. We looked out across the hillside of red brick homes (many of which are glorified shacks). "Do you see that yellow house over there?" There was only one house with any paint at all. "Yes, of course," I replied. "That's the home of the Rodriguez family . . . look over there too." He was pointing again, this time to the right. "That's where the Mendoza family lives. I'm from the Herrera family." Now he was pointing to the cluster of homes in the immediate surroundings. "Our families have been feuding for years. They killed my uncle, my brother, and a few others. Though I've never killed anyone, others from my family have."

"What started the violence?" I asked. "That's easy," Juan Carlos replied. "It started when Nike shoes were introduced to the barrio." Then he corrected himself. "No, it was when *Air Jordans* arrived. The Mendoza family killed my cousin for his shoes. We retaliated. It went back and forth. It started when I was twenty years old. I'm thirty-three now."

Juan Carlos needed no prompting to continue educating me. "If I made a list of my peers that have died because of this, there would be fifty names on it. Only ten from my generation are alive, and we're marked men. Last year they poisoned me with a drink. I should have died, but the Lord saved me."

Luis is a friend and Christian co-worker who was born and raised in San Pedro. He and Juan Carlos (see inserted story) went up to the barrio the day before a planned outreach there with a visiting youth group. They were looking for one of Juan Carlos' cousins, the leader of his family-based gang. They wanted to clear the way with the "local authorities" so the group wouldn't have problems the next day. What they encountered came as no surprise. Even so, seeing an altar to the angel of death in the *malandro* headquarters was a wakeup call for Luis. He asked Juan Carlos' cousin for permission to pray. The cousin, in a "what's-wrong-with-this-picture?" moment, gave Luis the green light to pray aloud to the God who wills an end to the devilish scheming to which that place was dedicated.

A threefold cord of deadly forces hangs like a noose around the neck of young men: drugs, demons, and revenge. Juan Carlos' family is caught up in a vicious cycle of revenge that has taken the lives of an entire generation of youngsters. His cousin's pact with the angel of death is to secure protection and increase his predatory prowess. Drugs bring income, momentary escape, and a gateway for demonic influences. Lies hold the noose of death in their grip. Principal among these is the myth that the problem of violence will be solved with violence.[1]

WHAT A YOUNG MAN DID—AND PAID FOR

> I'll never forget a conversation I had with a twenty-two-year-old man named Hedilson. It was 5:00 p.m. on a Friday afternoon. The community was gathered around the corpse of a young man who had been shot and killed. His blood lay splattered on a public walkway amid a few homes just a stone's throw from my front door.
>
> Hedilson and I stood no more than fifty feet from the young man's body. Hedilson did two years in jail for a street crime. While locked up, he experienced Christ's love and learned the truth of God's Word. Now Hedilson was settling down with a wife and newborn son. He was developing a reputation in the community for being *tranquilo* (easygoing, non-troublemaking). Yet Hedilson wasn't pursuing God.
>
> My teammate and I challenged Hedilson to make a full return to the Lord and to work with us in the community. With a young man's dead body directly behind us, it wasn't hard to talk

---

1. Wink, *Powers That Be*, 42–62, 145.

> straight about the need to work with the young people of the slum. But Hedilson balked. He said he wasn't ready.
>
> Four weeks later to the day, the same killer struck again. This time the victim was my new friend Hedilson. The murderer had threatened Hedilson's brother. Hedilson foolishly went to the young man to reason with him, only to get a bullet in his heart.
>
> We grieved for yet another fatherless child and shattered home, and the daunting prospects of making a difference in such a troubled and violent place.

For the relationally adept ones, there's another path. *Fit in!* This is the way of social navigation and negotiation. Luis took this path. He learned to accommodate to the different groups, finding ways to serve them while remaining neutral. This tactic only works if you're not blood-related to the feuding families. This posture enabled Luis to approach Juan Carlos' cousin the way he did.

Finally, some families do everything within their means to keep their kids locked away inside their home, safe from danger. These children go to school in the morning and come home in the afternoon, remaining essentially quarantined there. The thinking is, "I won't stick my nose in your business. If you do the same, the world will be a better off!" *Keep to yourself!*

What Is a Kid to Do? 105

Claudia, who has become a dear friend, feels the violence is out of control, and living in San Pedro unbearable. Her children are too much at risk. What's a disciple to do? What's her hope? What's the way of Jesus in this place?

13

What Are the Faithful to Do?

IN PART 1 I marked out how faithful Jews expressed hope for the restoration of their nation during the crisis of Jesus' era. These responses were to:

1. *Escape* to the outlying hills to await the "day of the Lord" (the Essenes)
2. *Fight* against Rome—their oppressor who robbed them of their God-given sovereignty (the Zealots)
3. *Accommodate* to the ways of Rome, using access to political and cultural influence in service of their nation (the Sadducees)
4. *Separate* from everything unclean and unworthy of Israel's identity as bearers of God's Law (the scribes and Pharisees)

These crisis-inspired, hope-driven options expressed the common longing for God's promised day of visitation when he would rule in peace and justice. The faithful differed in how they thought this would come about. The Essenes expected divine intervention. The Zealots became a guerrilla movement to take back God's promised land. The Sadducees made peace with their privileged role, justifying their relationship with Rome as their means of influencing Israel toward God's purposes. The scribes and Pharisees hoped to preserve the nation's identity through strict observance of the law. They likely had more in common with the Zealots than we normally think, since their concern for the Law was also a means of resisting Roman encroachment upon Israel's stature as God's people.

Given the expectation of God's vindication, it shouldn't be surprising that with the possible exception of the Sadducees, these paths considered their gentile occupiers to be the principle obstacle to God's will being done. The removal of the imperialists, even by force, was something God would have to do.

I've argued that Jesus didn't align himself with these movements but that he carved out a unique path. Jesus marked out the way of shalom, which was the way of the cross—a path that ultimately betrayed the logic of everyone.

I intentionally described barrio San Pedro's responses to the crisis of their community in direct parallel to the paths of first-century Palestinian Jews. In the slums, as in Jesus' time, people *escape* (hitting the road to get out of the slum), *fight* (overpowering each other to stay on top), *accommodate* (trying to fit in by navigating the conflictual environment), and *separate* (keeping to themselves in self-preservation). Unlike first-century Jews, the barrio residents respond to their crisis without the equivalent expectation of vindication.

WHAT THE FAITHFUL IN THE SLUMS DO

Knowing the ancient ways in Israel helps us see contemporary Christian responses for what they are. By making use of the interplay between the crisis paths of first-century Palestine and those of the barrios, we will see more clearly how Christians in the slums witness to the hope of the gospel, since the historical ways in Israel reveal how our responses today may or may not line up with the road marked out by the One we follow.

Nonresidential Christians (Escape)

Looking for greener pastures is a phenomenon as old as the hills, even if motivations for escaping vary. Moses fled Egypt as a fugitive from the law. His life was in danger. Even as a murderer with a cause, Moses was prepared by God during those years away and then called back to Egypt. Unlike Moses, the Essenes escaped as a strategy and belief in what they considered the most righteous way to await God's coming vindication.

For Christians in Caracas' slums, greener pastures are found in the countryside from where parents or grandparents came to the big city. For some, a safer area of Caracas is pursued, though always through family connections. Upon knowing Christ, many dream of something better for the first time. This kind of move is considered deliverance from the lion's den. The impulse for these moves is more a matter of survival than strategy, more akin to Moses' dilemma than to the Essenes' faith. This is the predicament in which Claudia and her family find themselves.

Che Meets Judas the Maccabaean (Fight)

In Latin America everyone knows Che. Ernesto ("Che") Guevara was an Argentine medical doctor who became a freedom fighter. He died in 1968 at the hands of the CIA while fighting the tyranny of U.S. imperialism in Bolivia. He lives on in the people as a symbol of the *lucha* ("struggle") for social justice and self-determination. As a bigger-than-life icon, Che is seen on T-shirts, posters, hats, street murals, and more. Artwork portrays him as a Christ figure, likening his death to Jesus' crucifixion.

Most Christians don't know Judas the Maccabaean. He lived about one hundred-seventy years before the birth of Christ. Though we might not know the man, most know the Jewish holiday he inspired. Hanukkah is a Jewish festival celebrated every December in remembrance of a guerrilla revolt in Palestine that drove out Israel's tyrannical enemies. Judas the Maccabaean was the leader of the rebellion, which dramatically renewed the Jews' confidence in God's vindication of them as his people. In the time of Jesus, he was still a living icon, a symbol that inspired a crisis-ridden Israel to believe in God's rescue from their pagan oppressors. The Zealots were inspired by his example.

Jesus didn't follow the way of Judas the Maccabaean. He didn't take up arms in his mission to fulfill God's purposes for Israel. He modeled, taught, and died a different way. If Che isn't an icon worthy of Christ's way of shalom, where do we find icons that inspire Christian sacrifice in ways that are congruent with Jesus and his cross?

Some Catholics point to Monseñor Oscar Romero of El Salvador who gave his life sacrificially and nonviolently for the common people of his nation in 1981. Evangelicals in Venezuela don't know him, nor would they respect him if they did. The search for an evangelical icon of Romero's status is in vain. A Colombian pastor was killed by the drug cartel for his unrelenting efforts to see the church bring change to their drug-controlled city. Yet few even remember the pastor's name. His sacrificial death hardly reached iconic-class levels in the imaginations of evangelicals. It seems the only way to achieve such influence among evangelicals is to become a popular recording artist.

"Listen to Me, Satan!" (Fight)

Many evangelicals in Latin America express a fighting spirit akin to Che's. They call themselves *guerreros para Cristo* ("warriors for Christ"). Their *batalla* ("battle") is against Satan and his emissaries. Most aren't concerned with social justice or earthly empires. They believe the frontlines of our struggle for God's victory will be won in prayer, which they pursue sacrificially. Monthly, if not weekly, all-night prayer vigils are common.

Living icons abound among the warriors for Jesus. *Listen to Me, Satan* is the title of a well-known book by Carlos Annacondia that is representative of the movement.

"Christians Lite" (Accomodate)

Four percent of Venezuelans attend Sunday mass. Recently I heard Catholics in our slum describe themselves as "Catholics lite." This is their way of saying they're nominal believers and marginal to the church. They believe in God and Jesus Christ while recognizing that their dedication to the faith is questionable. In practice, they're spiritually eclectic. They keep their options open, reserving the right to consult witches, sorcerers, and santeros to resolve their personal problems. This form of syncretism mixes Christianity with animistic practices.

There's no lack of inspirational icons for the "Christians lite." Two such figures sanctioned by the Catholic Church are José Gregorio Hernández and the "Nazareno de San Pablo." These figures inspire much devotion among "Catholics lite." Though endorsed by the church, their use in rituals is animistic in nature.

Like the Sadducees who accommodated to Rome's system, "Catholics lite" make peace with the ways of the ruling pagans, as it were. Yet unlike the Sadducees, whose deepest, historical identity was with the nation of Israel, there's a significant spiritist movement in Venezuela that lays claim to that deeper, historical sense of identity. They encourage Catholics to honor their indigenous (animistic) roots. From this perspective, "Catholics lite" accommodate to the later, foreign arrival of Roman Catholicism.

Successful Christians (Accommodate)

Evangelicals practice a different form of syncretism. They get seduced by the market orientation of their economically successful Christian brethren to the north. Latin American evangelicals believe that America's Protestant faith is blessed by God. By partaking in the same faith, these "successful Christians" hope to share in the same prosperity. If America's economic blessing is the result of their Protestant faith, then it stands to reason that the secrets to success are embedded in the faith they espouse. A quick perusal of pop Christian literature in American evangelical bookstores reveals the syncretism of "success principles" with the gospel. This literature becomes the meat and potatoes (or rice and beans!) of Latin American evangelicalism.

The symbols of "successful Christians" are a three-piece suit and a new car, or simply a business card. Icons are the young, polished pastors with big ministries and budgets who get notoriety from TV, music, and books. For believers from the slums, attending a "successful church" and being associated with a "successful pastor" meets a need for hope in the midst of the crisis they live in.

To the Catholic hierarchy, of course, this evangelical influence from the north represents a foreign threat to the cultural integrity and identity of the church. Each side, the successful evangelicals and the Catholic hierarchy, accuses the other of accommodating to the enemy.

The Separate Ones (Separate)

"Be holy, as I am holy." For this evangelical sector, holiness means living physically separate from the world and its influences. They feel under siege by the surrounding worldliness of their environment, which they consider the devil's playground. This plays wells with the social rule of the slums: "*No te metas con nadie.*" (Dynamically translated, "Don't stick your nose in anybody else's business!")

Within this social rule, there's room to wiggle. Believers like Claudia and Miguel don't have the option of keeping to themselves. Claudia is a caregiver. Her home is akin to Grand Central Station, with a steady stream of family and neighbors coming through to complain, confide, emote, or spread the latest community news (or to be informed of the same).

Unfortunately, the pull to separate is strong. When natural leaders like Claudia convert to Christ, they typically close the door to the community in their kitchen to be faithful to their new church community. To counter this with Claudia and Miguel, we keep formal meetings to a minimum by infusing gospel meaning into family gatherings for birthdays and holidays.

The "separate ones" understand the spiritual battle they are in. They hope in God's ultimate victory over the evil powers that overwhelm their community. Their spirituality is militaristic. They make forays out into the community to preach or hand out tracts, never lowering their guard before their neighbors or listeners. Their motto could be characterized as: "Take the offensive . . . give them the message." They then retreat to a safe place to regroup.

They have found a way of engaging the world, though in a rather forced and distant manner. Their hope is that God will rescue people from the barrio, giving them a better life in heaven. They expect God to honor their service and reward their valiant spirit. This is the hope that sustains them. They're the ones most likely to remain in the slums.

These descriptions function as a composite profile, since many believers identify to one degree or another with all of them. Several underlying impulses are worth noting: (1) the sense of being under the threat of outside forces; (2) the need to exercise power over their circumstances; and (3) the hope and expectation of God's blessing not only in the afterlife but also in the here and now.

Yet what vision for the barrios do these paths inspire? Where's the gospel of power in vulnerability? Claudia's questions remain, crying even louder for answers: What's a disciple to do? Where does she find her hope? What's the way of Jesus in her barrio?

14

What Did the Faithful One Do?

JESUS DIDN'T ESCAPE TO the hills, take up arms, seek power and position, or reinforce Israel's exclusive identity. His way was altogether different. In the groundbreaking treatise that marked his mission, Jesus trotted out what I like to call the preamble to the constitution of God's kingdom: the Beatitudes.

"Blessed are the poor, those who weep, the meek, those who hunger and thirst because they don't have justice/righteousness, the merciful, the pure of heart, the peacemakers, and the persecuted ones." This renewed Israel, with its new covenant and king, would possess God's kingdom, inherit the earth, be comforted, satisfied, forgiven, endowed with divine vision and character, and rewarded with God's highest praise.

With this simple, poetic declaration, Jesus left no doubts that his way was *not* the way of:

- retreat to safer ground (the way of the Essenes)
- revenge and violence (the way of the Zealots)
- positional power, titles and influence (the way of the Sadducees)
- ethnic and religious boundary-keeping (the way of the scribes and Pharisees)

The way of Jesus, according to the Beatitudes, revealed a different path, a kingdom of shalom. We unpacked this vision in part 1 with the help of the prodigal parable and the story of Caligallo the street criminal. There, as well as in the Beatitudes, this Jesus way is characterized by:

- the unlikely, weak, beaten-up people highly esteemed and uniquely affirmed
- relationships of love, peace, mercy, and justice in families, communities and nations

- heart devotion to God expressed in love for others, even at the risk of rejection and misunderstanding

Jesus didn't waste time before beginning his suffering-preparation program. He wanted the DNA of rejoicing in persecution to be foundational in the kingdom movement he fomented. Walking in the light of these kingdom truths would be risky business. He implied that some people wouldn't take a liking to unseemly, unworthy people living in love, forging peace between enemies, extending mercy on their fellow "bad people," and expecting justice from their nation's leaders. There was already a hint of the cross in this preliminary statement. From the start, Jesus carved out space "outside the gate" (Heb 13:12) where his followers would join him.

Recently I sat down with Claudia, Miguel, and other neighbors to read Scripture and pray. We dove into the Beatitudes, considering Jesus' strange vision for his future leaders. I say "strange" because it struck me that Jesus' listeners would have been predominantly men. Jesus called men to be meek and to cry. Looking across at Miguel, I voiced this. We pondered Jesus' words of blessing for the poor in spirit. For men, this is a counter-instinctive set of vision points. We held these "non-macho" perspectives in tension with discussion about the senseless violence that engulfs the barrios. The gospel, according to Jesus, implied a path that was out of step with family and neighbors.

I reminded them that Israel too lived in a state of crisis. Some fled to the hills. Others fought back. My friends shook their heads. They knew what that meant. We discussed how Christians from San Pedro don't worship in San Pedro. Why is that? Everyone wants to leave, they said. One couple, quite close to Claudia and Miguel, mentioned having discussed with Claudia and Miguel the possibility of moving somewhere together.

Later, the Holy Spirit taught our friends how to interpret Jesus' ways for their context. Claudia and another woman from the Bible study group were elected to leadership positions in the San Pedro neighborhood council. They immediately committed a Beatitude-like leadership act. They recruited an assistant to help them, an abused and despised woman whose infamy runs far and wide through the barrio. In Bible terminology, Ingrid is an "unclean" person, socially shunned by neighbors. As an assistant to our friends, she accompanies them on their house visits. This role gives her a honorable venue for restoring her dignity throughout the community. Claudia and her friend are joining Jesus "outside the gate," where the unworthy are saved and healed.

15

What Did the Apostle Do?

THE APOSTLE PAUL OFFERS another perspective on biblical hope and the way of Jesus. In Romans 5, Paul writes about how God saved us. He gets worked up about how gracious and free God acted in Christ to give us such a treasure.

"We rejoice in the hope of God's glory" (Rom 5:2). Paul expects hope (in God's glory) to produce a deep, emotional response within believers. To rejoice is more than lending intellectual assent to a fact. The heart gets involved, and not lightly. This matter of "hope in God's glory" is a big deal, or should be, according to Paul. It's something worth getting excited about. And that's not all.

"We also rejoice in our suffering" (Rom 5:3). The apostle says in effect that as believers, we're totally into this incredible gift of hope that God has given us in Christ. And guess what? We're also totally in step with God's unusual gift of troubles and suffering! Huh? That comes from left field. Isn't Paul talking out of both sides of his mouth? He claims that hope doesn't disappoint us (5:5), yet without the character and maturity that comes from suffering we can't hold on to this hope. What kind of suffering? Losses and disappointments, for starters. Certainly persecution and rejection too.

Somehow hope makes sense out of suffering. Hope provides a unique perspective on suffering. And this vision must be somehow earthy and concrete. It touches our hearts and affections, exerting the power to sustain and inspire us in adversity.

In 1 Thessalonians 1:3, Paul attributes endurance to hope ("endurance inspired by hope"). According to Romans 12:12, we are "patient in affliction" because our hope gives birth to joy and inspires the patience needed to suffer and continue believing and praying.

It feels like I'm sidestepping an "elephant in the room." I have hinted at the animal, alluding to its presence while trying to avoid stating the obvious. (After all, maybe I'm imagining the big thing?) What's the elephant? In a word, if I may be so direct, it's the cross, the way of Jesus—his unique, crisis-inspired path of discipleship that set him apart from all others.

AN EARTHY CROSS FOR EARTHY DISCIPLESHIP

Perhaps the elephant is more precisely the expectation (from God!) that we follow the same way, a proposition too concrete for comfort's sake. Let me explain. During our deepest engagement with Caligallo (chaps. 1–3), the streets were extremely "hot." Every team member got mugged or robbed more than once within a six-week period. Things got so bad that we broached the topic of whether it constitutes "dying for the gospel" if one of us gets killed. Some felt that, no, if a street thug randomly shoots one of us, it's not for the gospel since the assailant isn't persecuting us because of our faith. Others felt that our "yes" to the Lord and his call to serve in such a dangerous place made our lives an expression of faith. Therefore whether or not a street criminal targeted us as Christians, we would be giving our lives for the gospel.

Were we simply a traumatized bunch of Christian workers trying to find some comfort in uncomfortable circumstances? Or were we hinting at a deeper question, perhaps something profoundly relevant for Christian witness in violent places?

Without denying the influence of our traumatized state, I believe that we bumped into something more. We were wrestling with how our life and ministry in the streets of Caracas unite us in a tangible way to Jesus' death.

I'm not comfortable with this line of questioning. I don't know what to do with the apostle Paul's words in Colossians 1:24, "I rejoice in my sufferings for you, that in my flesh, I may complete what is lacking in Christ's afflictions." How am I to understand Paul's motivation "to know Christ . . . and the fellowship of sharing in his sufferings, becoming like him in his death" (Phil 3:10)? Does Paul suggest that Jesus' suffering on the cross continues today in the life of his body, the church?

I don't readily identify with Jesus' agony because the meaning I attribute to his death is spiritual and theological. I'm most at home proclaiming what I believe God accomplished through the cross. No doubt the lack of persecution and physical suffering in America enables the perpetuation of this bias.

Ironically, my bias stands in stark contrast with Jesus' most repeated call to discipleship: "If anyone would come after me, they must deny themselves and take up their cross and follow me" (Matt 16:24). This problem is to be expected when a leading evangelical voice writes, "What can be said . . . about the relationship between Christ's sacrifice and ours? I think we have to insist that they differ from one another too widely for it ever to be seemly to associate them."[1] We have been taught to adhere to a theological truth but not to the way of life implied by it.

We proclaim in public baptism that "we have been baptized into Jesus' death" and that "if we have been united to Christ in the likeness of his death, we will certainly be united to him also in his resurrection" (Rom 6:3). This is a passage about freedom—freedom from the sin that enslaved us, and from our ties to the first Adam. According to Paul, our old ways, apart from Christ and his kingdom, were put to death when Jesus died. In his death, all died (2 Cor 5:14). Christ's death set us free to love and serve others.

This truth fed my evangelical formation. Yet we can't stop here. We must keep the theological meaning linked with the historical, earthy Jesus. The spiritual union we dramatize in the waters of baptism must remain united in substance with the One who "endured such opposition from sinners" that he was rejected, persecuted, tried, and condemned to death as a criminal. We must hold together the *description* "we have all been baptized into his death" with the *prescription* "if anyone would come after me, they must . . . take up their cross and follow me." The former confirms our identity; the latter challenges it. Both speak of following Jesus and the fundamental vocation of the church as Christ's testifying body on earth.

Is there hope without suffering? When we look at the cross and the sorrow it points to, we are to see hope—not only eternal, but also in the here and now that inspires and sustains our labor for the Lord. So much so that Paul makes the audacious claim that he found joy in sharing Jesus' suffering.

This is what biblical hope does *to* us and *for* us—at least as the apostle thought it should. Now we'll look at the larger landscape of this

1. Stott, *Cross of Christ*, 273.

to discover the promise to which we hold firmly, and which had the power to inspire Paul and Jesus. If it inspired them, maybe it will also inspire disciples like Claudia and gospel workers like me.

16

Biblical Hope Revisited

> "But now, Lord, what do I look for? My *hope* is in you."
> (Ps 39:7)
>
> "Put your *hope* in God."
> (Ps 42:5)
>
> "Be strong and take heart, all you who *hope* in the Lord."
> (Ps 32:24)
>
> "A faith and knowledge resting on the *hope* of eternal life, which God, who does not lie, promised before the beginning of time."
> (Titus 1:2)

THE FUNDAMENTAL PROMISE TO which we hold is the promise of eternal life, a sure hope because it rests on God himself. Yet when I consider Claudia on the one hand and the cross on the other, the standard answers—God and eternal life—beckon me further. An honest life lived in the world demands it. Scripture also urges me deeper. Why? Because Claudia's hope is to leave San Pedro. She, like most believers in San Pedro, petitions God to get her out of the community.

If Claudia's hope is only eternal life, understood as going to heaven when she dies thanks to the forgiveness she has in Christ, then she has no compelling, biblical reason for staying in the barrio. Why risk her life, her family, and, if nothing else, her emotional well being if her faith is a ticket out of this world? What would constrain a disciple like Claudia to remain in her community for the sake of the gospel? What hope would inspire her to seek God's kingdom right where she is?

Perhaps if Claudia had more evangelistic passion, that would compel her to stay. Yet the gospel taught in the evangelical tradition hasn't accomplished this ideal. The lack of vision for the present, physical communities we occupy trumps evangelistic fervor. Why stay to evangelize when we can visit frequently to share the gospel? Without an inspiring purpose for a body of believers who live and breathe in the community, the zeal for evangelism quickly morphs into a transplanted, nonresidential task.

Our hope consists of God and his promise of eternal life. No question. Yet the pat explanations of our evangelical heritage don't suffice. Going into God's presence when we die is an essential part of the picture, but it's not enough. It falls short of biblical hope.

Because of this we must explore a biblical understanding of the hope and promise to which Jesus and the apostles attest. We'll do this by revisiting the familiar truths of eternal life, resurrection, new life, and glory, building on the historical paradigm presented in part 1.

ETERNAL LIFE FOR ISRAEL[1]

Jesus directed the message of eternal life to a group of people, not just individuals. Israel understood it as a message to them as a nation. They knew their need: deliverance from oppressors, sovereignty in their land, a just king, consolation in their hearts, and peace with their neighbors. As a nation suffering the loss of ancient symbols of identity (land, king, temple), the message of eternal life signified the end of their long season of exile, the new exodus out of bondage. It meant their restoration as a people in fulfillment of God's Word as spoken through the prophets. This was how Jesus viewed his message and mission to Israel.

Not all of Israel responded to that call. Individuals did, and perhaps whole families and social groups. As a people, however, Israel didn't say "yes" to Jesus as their Deliverer (John 1:11). The call remained, and those who responded saw themselves not as individual souls rescued by God but as firstfruits of God's fulfilling word to their people.

Peter's sermon at Pentecost illustrates this. "Therefore let all Israel be assured of this: God has made this Jesus, whom you crucified, both Lord and Christ" (Acts 2:36). What was the response to this message? The people were cut to the heart and responded as a group, crying,

---

1. Wright, *Challenge of Jesus*, 184.

"Brothers, what shall *we* do?" Peter called them to repentance and baptism, immediately giving them the vision of reaching the rest of their people. "The promise [of the Holy Spirit] is for you and your children and for all who are far off—for all whom the Lord our God will call" (v. 39). Peter's vision hadn't yet expanded to include gentiles. His phrase "all who are far off" indicated the rest of the nation.

ETERNAL LIFE FOR HUMANKIND

The message "God loves us" begs the question, who is *us*? To what collective identity do you and I belong? Who is "our people"? Our collective identity reaches back to creation: the human race, created in the image of God.

Paul's address to the Athenians echoes this: "God gives life and breath to *everyone* . . . in him we [humans] live and move and have our being . . . now God commands *all people everywhere* to repent . . . he has given proof of this to *all people* by raising [Christ] from the dead" (Acts 17:25–31). God's message through the apostle encompassed all humanity, not just the Athenians.

The parallelism between Paul's preaching among gentiles and Peter's among Jews is striking. Peter spoke a collective message to "all Israel," calling the nation into their God-given destiny and promise. Paul called the Athenians, as part of humanity, to take their rightful place in Christ, the second Adam. As God sent the Messiah to make good on what he promised to Israel—a restored nation according to its vocation—so God sent the *last* Adam to make good on what he designed in the beginning—a humanity true to its identity, destiny, and purpose as image-bearers of their Maker.

As God's image-bearers, we become God's renewed humanity. Ephesians 4:22 draws our attention to Genesis 1 with Paul's charge to "put on the new *human* [male and female], created to be like God in true righteousness and holiness." Colossians 3:10 expresses the "now and not yet" nature of this: "[You have] put on the new nature, which is being renewed in the knowledge of the image of its Creator." In Corinth, the apostle calls the gentile believers into their identification with Adam, the prototype of humankind in the creation story (1 Cor 15:22).

We're familiar with the idea that God has a covenant with Israel. We're not accustomed to the thought that God has a covenant with humanity and creation. Yet just as God renewed his covenant with Israel, calling her forth according to her vocation, so God made his creation covenant new by calling forth all peoples and nations to our original purpose. This affirms that Israel is to the Sinai covenant (Exod 19–20) as humanity is to the creation covenant (Gen 1:26–31).

Therefore there is a sequence to God's redemptive history. It began as broadly as possible with God creating the universe and humans to exercise his delegated dominion on earth. To fulfill this original design, God called Israel into being as a covenant partner. Thus from all creation God narrowed his project of restoration to one people, called to be instruments in bringing the rest of humanity to its fulfillment as image-bearers of our Creator.

God then narrowed things once more. He called forth his own Son, as representative of Israel *and* humanity, to fulfill the destiny of Israel *and* the human race. As we explored in part 1, Jesus fulfilled God's promises to Israel in a surprising and unacceptable way. The coming of Israel's promised king also marked the coming of humanity's new Adam (1 Cor 15:45–49). This affirms Jesus of Nazareth as the ultimate expression and truest testimony of Israel according to its calling *and* humankind according to its calling.

The Good News of eternal life is a message to humanity, calling us to our vocation as image-bearers of our Creator. This larger vision captures beautifully what it means to be saved, painting a much richer and fuller picture than the idea of individuals experiencing new life in Christ or Jesus as merely *personal* Savior.

Salvation for a Violent Barrio

God's Good News addressed to an entire slum, rather than just the individuals, alters the agenda of a simple home Bible study. Claudia and Miguel recently found another home in their neighborhood that was open to reading Scripture. A teammate and I joined them in facilitating the new group. To our surprise, the host couple knows people on both sides of the family feud in barrio San Pedro (see chapter 12). Their home, in fact, lies in the neutral zone of the community.

A woman from one of the feuding families came to this home to read Scripture with us. When the group was considering another home to gather in, someone suggested a neighbor living just up the staircase from the current meeting place. At this, the visiting woman responded, "If we do that, then I can't attend." "Why's that?" we asked, knowing the answer. "My family avoids all dealings with that family."

The group didn't move to the new home. But the woman from the proposed new home came down to join us the next week. There, in the simplicity of a small house gathering, representatives of two warring families began the hard work of dealing with each other. In the process, the entire group captured a gospel for the *barrio*, not just individuals of the barrio—a gospel of restored relationships, of peace and reconciliation, and a church *of* the community. Because the Bible-reading agenda was more than about getting individuals to make a confession of faith or following individual-focused discipleship steps, the Holy Spirit could lead us in a hope-inspiring, neighborly matter.

RESURRECTION REVISITED

Now we turn to Jesus' resurrection, the biblical anchor to our collective hope as humans in the new Adam.

> A: In the beginning God created the heavens and the earth.
> B: In the beginning was the Word.
>
> A: The earth was formless and empty; darkness was over the surface of the deep.
> B: The light shone in the darkness, but the darkness did not overcome it.
>
> A: And God said: "Let there be light," and there was light.
> B: The true light that gives light to everyone was coming into the world.
>
> A: Let us make humans in our image.
> B: He came to his own, but his own did not receive him.
>
> A: God blessed them and said: "Be fruitful and increase in number; fill the earth and subdue it."
> B: Peace be with you! As the Father sent me, so I send you.

A: God breathed into his nostrils the breath of life.
B: Jesus breathed on the disciples and said: "Receive the Holy Spirit."

This antiphonal reading underscores an intriguing link between the Gospel of John and the book of Genesis.[2] "In the beginning": the first words off John's pen and the first lines of Holy Scripture. Genesis begins with God's work of creation. Day one, God speaks light into being. Day two, the sky. Day three, land. On day six, God creates humankind in his own image, then rests on the seventh.

John's Gospel begins with Christ the "Word" who was with God "in the beginning," through whom all things were made—an explicit allusion to creation. In Genesis 1, God's creating work finishes on day six. In John 19:30–31, on "the day of preparation" (preparation for day seven, the Sabbath), Jesus cries out, "It is finished" and dies. His work is completed on day six. In Genesis, God rests on day seven. In John, the Christ "rests" in the tomb on the seventh day.

> Early on the *first day of the week*, while it was still dark, Mary Magdalene went to the tomb and saw that the stone had been removed. (John 20:1)
> On the evening of that *first day of the week*, when the disciples were together, with the doors locked for fear of the Jews, Jesus came and stood among them and said, "Peace be with you!" After this he showed them his hands and side. (John 20:19–20)

John's use of "the first day of the week" in the resurrection narrative doesn't appear coincidental. The apostle wants us to notice something. He points to a Savior who was in the beginning, through whom all things were created, and who rose on the first day of the week. This is biblical "code language": Jesus' resurrection is the first day of God's new creation! Easter morning is the birthday of God's new world.

What does this have to do with hope? The newness birthed at Easter is more than new life granted to individuals, much more than personal salvation. Christ's rising as day one of his new creation gives us a much bigger window into God's gift of hope.

Creation, as recorded in the book of Genesis, encompasses the heavens and earth, and humankind made in God's image. The scriptural witness to "new creation," by implication, includes the concepts of "new humanity" and "new heavens and new earth." Paul writes of "new cre-

---

2. Wright, *Following Jesus*, 34–35.

ation" to the Galatians (6:15) and Corinthians (2 Cor 5:17). The prophet Isaiah and the apostles Peter and John speak of God's promise of "new heavens and a new earth" (Isa 65:17–25; 2 Pet 3:1–13; Rev 21:1–5). In God's new creation, through Jesus the crucified and resurrected One—the new Adam—we have the firstfruits of God's "new humanity" (1 Cor 15:45–49).

Late, Great Planet Earth?

This biblical exploration raises an important question: Where will we spend eternity? According to most sermons we hear, the answer is "heaven." According to the apostle John, the answer is earth. Though we might differ about what, when, and how the future will unfold in the end times, we can agree on how the story ultimately ends: the "New Jerusalem comes down out of heaven," and "the dwelling of God is with humans" (Rev 21:1–5).

If that question doesn't rattle us enough, here's another: Is this terrestrial ball we currently occupy destined for the proverbial junkyard? Will it burn up as we escape with Jesus to God's presence? Let's take a look at a passage used to teach this view:

> In the last days scoffers will come . . . they will say, "where is this 'coming' he promised? . . . but they deliberately forget that long ago by God's word the heavens existed and the earth was formed out of water and by water. By these waters also the world of that time was deluged and destroyed. By the same word the present heavens and earth are reserved for fire, being kept for the day of judgment and destruction of ungodly people. But do not forget this one thing, dear friends: With the Lord a day is like a thousand years, and a thousand years are like a day. The Lord is not slow in keeping his promise, as some understand slowness. He is patient with you, not wanting anyone to perish, but everyone to come to repentance. But the day of the Lord will come like a thief. The heavens will disappear with a roar; the elements will be destroyed by fire, and the earth and everything in it will be laid bare. Since everything will be destroyed in this way, what kind of people ought you to be? You ought to live holy and godly lives as you look forward to the day of God and speed its coming. That day will bring about the destruction of the heavens by fire, and the elements will melt in the heat. But in keeping with his prom-

> ise we are looking forward to a new heaven and a new earth, the home of righteousness. (2 Pet 3:3–13)

Malachi 3:1–3 is the backdrop to this passage: "But who can endure the day of his coming? Who can stand when he appears? For he will be like a refiner's fire or a launderer's soap. He will sit as a refiner and purifier of silver . . . and gold." The fire referred to in 2 Peter 3 is a refiner's fire that burns up the dross and purifies the silver. The fire is for the "destruction of ungodly people" (v. 7), the "elements" (v. 10), and the heavens (v. 12).

The parallel between God's interventions, past and future, is curious. In Noah's case, God used water. In God's coming judgment, he'll use "fire." Both are biblical images of judgment, purification, and renewal. Both are elements from God's creation. In the Genesis account of the flood, the rains "destroyed" the earth. Was the earth's physicality eliminated? In fact, God didn't throw away one world and start over with a new one. Even though the earth was "destroyed" through the flood, it was the same material earth that emerged from the receding waters—no doubt greatly altered by the powerful effect of the rains. People died in judgment. Plant life and animal life perished. In bringing judgment and renewal, the waters accomplished God's intentions.

Peter seems to envision a similar kind of "destruction" in the planet's future. "Fire," like water, is part of God's creation and an image of how God brings judgment *and* renewal. Even though God's future judgment will be unmatched in magnitude, Peter doesn't give us any reason to think that the "destruction" of the earth, the heavens, the "elements," and "ungodly people" will eliminate, or "junk," what we know as the earth and the heavens. The terms "burning up," "laid bare," and "destroyed" all point to the same divine yet earthy act of renewing through purification and judgment. I say "earthy" because like rainwater, the "fire" is recognizable as something from God's creation, used as God's instrument.

This brings us again to the parallel with Noah. As Noah and his family survived in the ark, so those who are ready for that day will "weather it," even welcoming its coming. This implies they (we?) will be present in the midst of this incredible event.

Curiously, other passages like Isaiah 65:17, Revelation 21:1, and Matthew 24:35 imply a complete break between the original earth and what is to come.

> "Behold, I will create new heavens and a new earth. *The former things will not be remembered, nor will they come to mind.*" (Isa 65:17)

> "Then I saw a new heaven and a new earth, for the first heaven and the first earth *had passed away.*" (Rev 21:1)

> "Heaven and earth *will pass away*, but my words will never pass away." (Matt 24:35)

Do these passages teach that the world we live in will be replaced by a completely new earth? In my view, their poetic language conveys the idea of a drastic break, a complete transformation, though not necessarily a replacement of the present earth and heavens. No one knows how God will make all things new. The Bible doesn't provide that kind of exactitude. There's no way to avoid the tension and dynamism between replacement and renewal, continuity and discontinuity.

It does seems that this cataclysmic, apocalyptic event will somehow make sense from what we know of creation today. The apostle Paul describes the continuity between this age and the age to come as that of a plant that grows from a seed, "the body that is sown is perishable, it is raised imperishable" (1 Cor 15:37–44). When he continues, "if there is a natural body, there is also a spiritual body" (v. 44), we should imagine Jesus' resurrected body, the first "spiritual body" of the age to come, and the kind that will inhabit God's new earth.

The most compelling reason for believing in this kind of continuity is, in fact, the resurrected body of Jesus. In the glorified body of the Crucified One, we see what *newness* looks like—God's rendition of old and new, the original and the restored (John 20:26–27). The signs of suffering and judgment from his time of earth—nail scarred hands and pierced side—are visibly present, though healed and carried over into his new, heavenly body (1 Cor 15:40).

This has a tremendous impact on how we walk in hope. This points beyond our suffering and pain, past the cross we bear, and declares to Claudia and mission workers alike: your losses and afflictions won't be wasted. They'll be transformed.

As firstfruits of the new humanity (1 Cor 15:20–23), Jesus' resurrected body is the prototype of when "all will be made alive" and therefore, I believe, the principle grid for interpreting the discontinuity conveyed in Revelation 21:1, Isaiah 65:17 and Matthew 24:35.

THE HOPE OF GLORY REVISITED

This message of hope—God's promise of eternal life, salvation, redemption, deliverance, restoration, shalom, new creation, resurrection, however you wish to call it—includes humankind, planet earth, and the cosmos! All creation! Nothing God made falls beyond the reach of what Christ redeemed.

Paul might have had this in mind when he penned "the glorious riches of this mystery among the gentiles, that is Christ in you [plural], the hope of glory" (Col 1:27). This verse typically reinforces a reductionist theology that encourages us to be confident of going to heaven when we die. Yet to limit "glory" to the glorified state of individual souls appears out of character with the biblical witness we've explored. "Hope of glory" is stacked full of inspiring biblical substance. By the Spirit, Christ—the new humanity, the true Adam—is in the church as firstfruits of God's new creation, a sign to the world of God's promised shalom.

As Jesus' death and exaltation approached, he declared, "The hour has come for the Son of Man to be glorified" (John 12:23). Was Jesus declaring his body-made-new-in-resurrection power as firstfruits of God's new creation? I believe so.

This means that the cross points to new creation. Hebrews 13:12–13 underscores this. After declaring that Jesus' death "outside the city gate" has made us holy, the writer of Hebrews calls his readers to join the Lord there: "Let us, then, go to him outside the camp." What for? To "bear the disgrace he bore." This isn't cool. Not attractive in the least. What would motivate us to suffer like that? The promise of the new creation.

"For here we do not have an enduring city, but we are looking for the city that is to come." That city, of course, is the "new Jerusalem," yet another biblical image of newness. The character of "outside the gate" is the character of heaven, the eternal city. The city we look forward to will be a city marked by the Lord's shalom, where love and power, humility and majesty, the lion and the lamb come together in perfect harmony and truth. That realm beyond the city gate represents the City that endures, the place without walls. There will be unity between enemies, and God's people will live in openness, honesty, and vulnerability without shame or fear. Imagine the father's party, with both sons kicking up their heels, dancing in the joy of their broken relationship made new.

17

Partners in New Creation

As I write, the season of Lent is fast upon us, one that Catholics highly revere and evangelicals all but ignore. As a straddler, I live in both worlds, mentoring and teaching evangelicals while collaborating with the local parish in the traditional *via cruces* procession. Personally, I've always had mixed feelings about these forty days, never sure how to make them special. This year could be different. Perhaps it's fitting to walk with Claudia in her crisis of hope while journeying with Jesus on his road of suffering.

On the road to Calvary, Jesus didn't travel with a smile. He didn't want to suffer. The path was grim, and the prospects ugly. He even wavered in the garden. The crucifixion was that foreboding. It's safe to say he didn't feel "fulfilled" or "empowered" according to today's prevailing "laws of leadership" (sarcasm aside). The hope that Jesus clung to, or rather clung to him in his weakened state, was his vindication—nothing else, no other vision. And it didn't fail him. His heavenly father received the obedience he offered in the face of afflictions "endured . . . from sinful men" (Heb 12:3; Matt 16:21) and raised him in resurrection triumph—an artistic work in contrasts, and the ultimate signpost of our hope.

CUP HALF EMPTY

As a master painter utilizes distinct colors and shades to accentuate contrasting hues on a canvas, so "God demonstrated his love for us, in that while we were still sinners, Christ died for us" (Rom 5:8). These polar opposites are nowhere more aptly depicted than in the parable of the prodigal, between the heartbreaking insults and disgracing acts of the sons, and in the father's incomprehensible capacity to love, forgive, and restore shalom. An extraordinary study in extremes.

This pattern gets played out many times in Scripture. The Old Testament reads as a litany of mess ups. Abraham lied to the Egyptians about his wife, Sarah, saying she was his sister. He then went along with Sarah's encouragement to fulfill God's promise by having a baby with Hagar, their maidservant. Abraham's son Isaac, the child of promise, intended to impart his final blessing upon Esau, his firstborn. Through a scheming act of deception, Jacob received Isaac's blessing against his father's will.

These are the folks whose portraits decorate the "hall of faith" (Heb 11). Subsequent generations only got worse. Jacob's beloved son, Joseph, was almost killed by his brothers only to be sold into slavery in Egypt.

Granted, God is the hero of the story. But look what he does as hero. God takes our utterly inept efforts and accomplishes his divine purposes, receiving our part and transforming it into the fulfillment of his promises.

My faithfulness hasn't been photogenic. For many years I wasn't ready to learn from the people God brought into my life. Raised as a rugged individualist, without a father and under the tutelage of a hardworking mother who showed her love through actions more than words, I didn't learn to know my heart. My pride and false ideas about myself prevented me from opening up and acknowledging my needs. I experienced a faith crisis shortly after marrying at the age of twenty-eight. A dark cloud of troubling doubt hovered over me for months, and I refused to talk about it with anyone. It was my secret, and it could have been my downfall if not for God's grace.

Now I see this personal crisis as a God-given opportunity to open up with others about my real self. Fast forward fifteen years. After getting held up at gunpoint in Caracas, my pride finally conceded. For the first time in more than forty years, I considered my circumstances "acceptable" for meeting with a therapist. All this to say, the Lord exercised much patience with me, and my part in God's work has been plagued by more than my share of shortcomings.

We should be encouraged that the weight of Scripture doesn't fall on effective men and women who advance God's purposes on the earth. It pronounces God able to fulfill his promises in spite of us. Consider how many lessons Peter needed from Jesus, followed by divine revelations after Pentecost, to finally accept an uncircumcised gentile as a brother and God as Lord of the nations. The Holy Spirit worked sovereignly, giving Peter no choice in the matter (Acts 10:44). Not a strong case for God using him at his best.

This pattern is nowhere more drummed into our biblical thinking than in the post-resurrection early church. In Acts we read five times that "you crucified him . . . and God raised him from the dead" (Acts 2:23–24; 3:13–15; 4:10; 10:39; 13:28–30). In other words, "You screwed up big time, but God came through and saved the day—in a big way!"

Some might think this makes little of our part, or that we shouldn't try to succeed in ministry. In a discussion not unlike this, the apostle Paul anticipated his readers' reaction to God's wonderful reversing work (how God took our failure to be righteous in Adam and made us righteous in Christ) with the oft-quoted rhetorical question, "Should we therefore sin, so that grace may abound even more" (Rom 6:1)?

As Paul argued, this isn't a license to sin or a pretext to settle for failure in ministry. In fact, the examples I've held up reveal faithful men and women who followed God (Abraham and Sarah) and zealously sought Yahweh's will (the leaders who wanted Jesus dead). Peter followed Jesus to the end, believing himself brave. He was no vagabond looking for the easy way out. Peter wanted to be faithful. Israel's leaders manipulated the crowds at Jesus' sentencing in faithfulness to their God and nation. God's reversing work overcame Peter's cowardice, the Jewish high council's blind leadership, and the multitude's vulnerability. None of the above were rebellious sinners or faithless leaders. They had godly intentions and wanted to be used by God.

I've often wondered how anyone in Latin America could follow a religion that committed such atrocities in God's name. Yet we can praise God for what he's done in spite of the culturally-captive explorers that opened up the region. In all its gory, bloody tragedy, Latin America towers as a historic testimony to God's ability to take his people's shameful follies and call forth a people unto himself.

This is one side of the equation—the rather negative though necessary part. I say necessary because we can't count on ever "getting it right." We need to know that our Savior will win the day, come what may.

CUP HALF FULL[1]

The other, highly positive dimension of our part is this: by faith, our human actions of *new creation character* will remain. How can I claim that my act of loving an enemy or caring for the poor will form part of God's great, eternal shalom fest? Because of Jesus, the church's foundation, who resides outside the gate. According to Hebrews 13:12–14, Christ's sacrifice for sinners didn't belong to the current Jerusalem but to the "city that is to come." Our charge to join Jesus outside the camp stands on the compelling vision of the New Jerusalem, the glorious transformation of all things. According to the apostle Paul, the Jerusalem above is our "mother," a birthing that reveals where our works come from and where they will go (Gal 4:26).

In a variety of ways, Scripture alludes to the continuity between our labors here and the world to come, and how what we do carries over. In a plea for unity, the apostle Paul wrote this to the factious Corinthian congregation:

> If anyone builds on this foundation using gold, silver, costly stones, wood, hay, or straw, their work will be shown for what it is, because the Day will bring it to light. It will be revealed with fire, and the fire will test the quality of each person's work. If what they have built *survives*, they will receive their *reward*. If it is burned up, they will suffer loss; being saved themselves, but only as one escaping through the flames." (1 Cor 3:12–15; emphases mine)

In the day of judgment, our work will be tested. What we "build" in our earthly service to the Lord may "survive." According to Paul, if our work survives, we'll receive a reward. In Latin America, the topic of rewards is quite common in evangelical churches. In my background, to motivate Christians with talk of heavenly rewards was highly suspect, smacking of manipulative motivational tactics to get the flock to do more for the church. It surely couldn't breed anything good, selfless, or Christlike.

We need to rethink this. Jesus and the apostles speak of rewards attached to actions. "If anyone gives even a cup of water to one of these little ones because he is my disciple, I tell you the truth, he will certainly not lose his reward" (Matt 10:42). In the context of Matthew 10, Jesus

---

1. Bonino, *Doing Theology*, 142.

emphasizes that all God-honoring labors, big and small, will be rewarded. Significantly, the rewards highlighted in Matthew 10 tie directly into Jesus and his faithfulness. The deeds rewarded are those of "taking up our cross" and following Jesus in his offensive way marked by opposition, rejection, and persecution (10:37–39).

Thus our works survive when they prove true to Christ's faithful new creation work of giving himself up in "costly demonstrations of unexpected love." This, it seems, is the criteria for what burns up and what survives. Somehow these works carry over to the new order of things, perfected no doubt through God's purifying fire.

The apostles Paul and John write, "Each person will give an account of him or herself to God," and "My reward is with me, and I will give to everyone according to what they have done" (Rom 14:12; Rev 22:12). Many of us avoid these verses because they're so easily hijacked by the stern, wrathful image of a God intent on fault-finding and punishing. Yet from what we've explored, we can read these passages in a new light. They are in fact positive, and they affirm God's concern for Christlike obedience in our lives and the importance he places on our deeds in light of eternity.

In Romans 14, Paul challenges the church to mindfully walk in communion with fellow believers who are weaker or see things differently, a beautiful expression of breaking down walls that separate and seeking peace with one another. John's challenge also reveals the importance of our labors: what we do has eternal signficance.

For evangelicals within a narrow paradigm of Jesus the personal Savior, this becomes those activities narrowly defined as "spiritual." Thus the "spiritual" act of telling someone to follow Jesus will endure, while the "social" work of loving a lonely person by offering a listening ear bears no eternal consequence.

Yet this isn't the witness of Scripture. Nor is it inconsequential that those privileged to rule with the Lord in the first resurrection, during Christ's thousand-year reign, are those who literally lost their heads for the gospel. Martyrs who joined their Master "outside the gate" understandably receive special honor and a unique role. It's the *new creation character* of their Christlike obedience that will characterize the heavenly, eternal kingdom (Rev 20:4–6). We, therefore, have been charged to pursue the deeds, like Jesus', that demonstrate the new world of the resurrection.

Paul expresses this continuity in the "love chaper," 1 Corinthians 13:

> Love never fails. But where there are prophecies, they will cease . . . for we know in part and we prophecy in part, but when perfection comes, the imperfect disappears . . . now these three remain: faith, hope, and love. But the greatest of these is love."

In this overly-familiar passage, Paul's vision of the age to come inspires us to love. "Love never fails" because love belongs to the future realm of "perfection." Faith, hope, and love "remain" in the sense that they consist of kingdom substance that survives, that continues into that day when we will "see face to face."

Continuity and carryover are evident in other dimensions of the New Jerusalem. Revelation 21:23–24 speaks of nations (ethnic groups known today?) walking together, reconciled, in the light of the Lamb, and kings (heads of state?) "bringing their splendor into it" (servant leaders who trust rather than war against each other). Some kind of ongoing "healing of the nations" will occur there too (22:2), implying unfinished business from this side of eternity.

Thus far I've pointed an arrow toward God's future, arguing that our earthly works today can survive and form part of God's new creation. The other side of this truth is an arrow shooting from eternity back to the present. Our works survive precisely because they represent the inbreaking of God's future reign into our present age. In this sense, our new-creation works are ends in themselves, not merely means.[2] They survive because they contain the substance of the future, God's kingdom manifest now. They are God's renewed humanity making a home in the here and now, though tentative and spotty. This is the nature of a sign. A sign reveals a taste of heaven on earth and points our earthly existence toward heaven.

Jesus' resurrected body, not surprisingly, has much to do with this whole discussion. For in his nail scarred hands made new, we find the prototype of continuity between this age and the age to come. We catch a gliimpse of what the "surviving" of this age will look like. We see the present projected into the future and the future penetrating the present.

Curiously, the eternal identity of Christ, as attested to in John's Revelation, is that of the Lamb that was slain. This title was attributed

---

2. Ellul, *Presence of the Kingdom*, 49–78.

to him during his earthly mission as demonstrative of his death *and* of the ministry that led to his crucifixion. Only the character of Christ the Lamb, manifested throughout his kingly realm—past, present, and future—will produce a world without "death or mourning or crying or pain" (Rev 21:4).

STRANGE PARTNERS[3]

Hope, then, requires several interlocking components: a confidence in God's ultimate intervention in history that will finish Satan, sin, and death to fulfill his promise of making all things new, and an appreciation for the significance of human participation and how God uses our labors to usher in his new creation.

Israel's deliverance from slavery in Egypt captures these elements well. Moses, raised in Pharaoh's palace with all the royal privileges of the day, renounced his ties to the pagan throne to stand with the Hebrew slaves ("outside the gate," we might say) and work for their liberation. God, for his part, stepped into history and set his people free with a mighty hand (using a reluctant leader with a limited skill set and even less faith). The Hebrews stood before the Red Sea with the angel of the Lord behind them to protect them from Pharaoh's army. They had nowhere to go but forward. God didn't tell the angel to divide the sea. Nor did God act unilaterally. The rod of authority was placed in Moses' hand. Unlikely partners, yes, but partners they were, in divine, earthly deliverance.

Consider Peter's participation in launching the church at Pentecost. He denied his Lord three times, setting the stage for divine intervention that reversed his cowardly acts. Jesus pursued Peter, restoring him and entrusting him with shepherding responsibilities. Did Peter become the leader of the resurrection community because of his impeccable record of godly service? Did he successfully complete the Master's leadership training program? Peter didn't "take up his cross" as his Teacher taught him. He didn't follow Jesus "effectively" or "proactively" in his hour of suffering. God's kingdom came on the day of Pentecost in spite of Peter and the uninspired apostles. God's promise proved bigger than their in-

---

3. Mangalwadi, *Truth and Social Reform*, 124–39.

capacities. In the end, Peter's firsthand experience of grace in his hour of defeat was the lesson he needed to become lead pastor.

On the positive side of the equation, Peter's humility in leadership and power in ministry dramatically continued and expanded his Lord's mission. Eventually, the Jerusalem-based apostle came to a point of also suffering as his Master did—but only after failing once again, this time shrinking back from public association with "unclean," "uncircumcised" gentile brothers and sisters. Peter, as Paul's charge could be described, wasn't willing to "bear the disgrace Christ bore" (Gal 2:11–16; Heb 13:13). Experiences such as this no doubt taught the apostle much humility and wisdom for his critical role in leadership and enabled him to finish well as a vital, if unexpected, partner of God.

On a much smaller scale, recently five people were gunned down at a late-night party near Claudia's house. I recruited Juan Carlos (see chap. 12) to take the church youth to the home of the traumatized woman who hosted the bloodbath. Only after the visit did Juan Carlos realize that the woman was from a rival clan, the archenemies of his family. He had unknowingly entered his enemy's home as a minister of peace. It was a strange beginning to, and an unexpected partnership in, peacemaking in barrio San Pedro.

Biblical hope, voiced through local disciples and mission workers, declares confidently that Christlike obedience in the slums, "successes" and "failures" alike, is worth it. In God's hands this faithfulness becomes the substance with which God transforms this world into his new creation. The hope that inspires us to endure difficulties and tragedies is *more* than the faith to see God's eternal age of shalom. We also esteem our God-given role of bringing his promised deliverance to fruition.

We normally assume God will do more through us alive than dead. Biblical hope, courageously embraced, holds this assumption lightly, since nothing is too big or too bad for God's reversing work. No tragedy will be greater than God's victory, hidden as it might be for a time. All such afflictions and setbacks find their home in the long shadow of Jesus' cross and the Father's vindication on the third day. There our ugliest shortcomings are overcome by God's greatest reversal. There too our Christlike acts of peacemaking with our adversaries take their rightful place in the age to come.

A HOPEFUL WAY

During this Lenten season I am contemplating Christ on trial, seated before Pilate. Pilate elicits only snippets of information from his prisoner: "So you are a king?"

"That's what you say," responds Jesus. "This is why I've come into the world. To give testimony to the truth."

Christ, awaiting his sentence and pending execution, stands as a testimony to ultimate truth. Jesus, in that moment, becomes a picture of true hope. He believes in God's victory-to-be. No one present has the eyes to see it. Only Jesus. He hasn't lost sight of God's purposes. He knows who holds the ultimate authority in spite of appearances. He trusts his heavenly Father to act as Lord of history.

Jesus also knows his obedience reveals to the world the very nature of God: the lover of humanity, caring for us to the end, a sign of eternity. His "defeat" in the hands of sinners reveals God's victory—the firstfruits of all things new.

This hope-filled spirituality exudes freedom to fail but not to sit on the sidelines. God calls, "Take up the rod, Moses!" Jesus challenges, "Do you love me?" In my fears, whether peacemaking in the streets of Caracas or in my own heart, the Lord's gracious voice beckons me forward, "Come here where I stand. Behold my nail scarred hands made new . . . at the cliff's edge, in Cornelius' house, outside the gate. I don't want you to miss the party!"

At the end of the day, many questions remain. Answers, like a moving target, evade platitudes, even while pressing deeper in search of a resting place in my heart. As Venezuelans like to say, I have pointed to a *norte*—a point of reference, a northward compass, a picture of the God to whom we *stick*. I've also locked my sights on a gospel with the power to birth a church of witnesses (read *martyrs*) emboldened with the challenging, offensive hope of a kingdom worth living and dying for. This is an inspiring kingdom "outside the gate" with Christ and his resurrected nail scars, where as partners in new creation we stand with him, united as one—rich with poor, friend with foe, Jew with gentile, saint with sinner.

Afterword

SIX MONTHS BEFORE STARTING this writing project, I sat with my team in Caracas to read a letter from my friend and InnerCHANGE colleague, Nate Bacon. His letter was directed to the entire InnerCHANGE community serving in twelve cities worldwide. As part of our formation, we orchestrate collective learning around what we call our "Three Currents": missionary, prophetic, and contemplative. Nate's epistle introduced a series of readings on the "Prophetic Current." The following is an excerpt:

> In InnerCHANGE we are invited into intimacy with Jesus, especially through our friendship with the poor and marginalized. It is him we seek there, and his friendship, which we are privileged to receive as we are welcomed into deeper fellowship with our sisters and brothers on the margins. For those of us from the dominant class and the wealthier nations, this process is not unlike that of conversion.
>
> The anniversary of the Martyrdom of Archbishop Oscar Romero of El Salvador rested up against Easter this year, occurring the very next day. Romero's friendship with one of the first priests to be martyred at that time led him on his own "downward journey" and into intimate friendship with the poor and suffering Christ present among the Salvadoran people. He was truly converted to the poor: this shy, bookish member of El Salvador's comfortable class became a fiery prophet who announced the gospel and denounced injustice, torture, oppression, and killing.

When I came to the end of the letter, I paused long enough to make eye contact with each team member and to prepare my next words. "In this letter I see my life work." I had everyone's attention. "I can say it in two words." Was it my imagination, or was everyone on the edge of their seats? "My life work is to . . . prepare martyrs." Silence . . . then some more. When you're a twenty-five-year-old North American living in a dangerous Latin American slum and only six months into a three-year commitment, you don't want to hear your team leader say this kind of thing.

The silence finally broke. Someone laughed uneasily. They were digesting the bomb that detonated in each gut. I threw them a lifeline. "What I mean is . . . I want my ministry to equip people to love at great personal cost." In the end, I offered Jesus' metaphor for Christlike discipleship: "I want to inspire people to 'take up their cross,' which I believe means following Jesus and doing his works, even in the face of opposition and danger."

I tell this anecdote as an afterword because I did *not* set out to write about preparing martyrs. I was *not* conscious of what I was doing. Nor would I have wanted to introduce the book with such a bold declaration. Curiously, in the end, this is the very thing I articulated.

It's no secret that militaries prepare men and women to die, something I encountered personally in the sacrifice my dad made for America. In contrast to this, I want to see a different kind of "Greatest Generation" rise up that turns from nationalistic sacrifice to freely give itself in compassion to those "outside the gate" of family, community, and nation for the sake of God's shalom fest.

Once I completed the writing process, I synthesized my theologizing in the diagram below. The cross is positioned "outside the city gate," where God's new creation is manifest ("New Jerusalem" being representative of "all things new"). The two stick figures linked through the cross symbolize the father's heartbreaking sons or any one of us meeting and reconciling with God and an adversary. Inside the circle, "Jerusalem" is representative of Israel's national symbols, which provide the historical and covenantal foundation for how God is bringing history to fulfillment. The poetic stanzas enhance the diagram, further pulling together the many threads found in the book.

My friend and colaborer Nate ended his letter with a prayer that I offer to my readers as well:

> Let us ask God for the grace to open our hearts to be challenged and shepherded beyond our prejudices and fears . . . and may that love and that encounter transform us . . . into fiery prophets worthy of the name of our Lord Jesus. Amen.

Appendix

Some Thoughts on Teaching a Nail Scarred Hands Made New Gospel

GOD'S _____ LOVE

THE CENTRALITY OF TEACHING and living God's love can't be overstated. How we see God and the gospel is foundational. Everything builds on this. This "seeing" is experiential and conceptual. The theology on this point has already been explored, where I describe God's love with adjectives like "shocking," "unexpected," "costly," and "foolish" to recapture fresh visions of how God has loved us. The parables of Luke 15, with cultural insights from Kenneth Bailey, introduce a solid, biblical image of God. They also provide historical foundations since Jesus used them as commentary on his mission and conflict with Israel's leaders. Through these parables, new believers see how the father's humiliations dramatize Jesus' suffering on the cross.

God's love must also be experienced in community. We set the tone by telling our own stories in honesty and openness. This creates a safe space for new believers to open up and taste God's grace without shame. Our service must demonstrate a love grounded in freedom and gratitude without the compulsiveness and drivenness born out of guilt and people pleasing. The life we live is the message we teach.

A genuine experience with God's love thrusts new believers into the challenging world of engaging their neighbors. Concretely, the prodigal's father beckons them forth with open ears and minds toward their adversaries. Pushing this even further, Caligallo, representative of street criminals, becomes their teacher, the one who exposes their prejudice and uncomfortably calls them to overcome it. Not an easy proposition. Here's one way to articulate this love-your-neighbor challenge:

- Who comes to mind when I think of people my *friends* would never want me to reach out to in love and respect?
- Who would my *parents* wish me to stay away from?
- Is there a *nation* or group that represents a betrayal of loyalty to my country if I were to reach out to them with Christ's love and respect?

Loving those my loved ones don't is difficult, though Christlike. As children of God the peacemaker, we too seek peace (Matt 5:9). We too party with both sons, since we're sent as Christ was (John 20:21). This is the offense of Jesus' primacy that relativizes every counterfeit absolute. It's also the scandal my neighbors faced in the challenge to see themselves as no different from Caligallo.

Our presence in the slums contributes to overcoming this challenge. We function as a sign that begs for explanation ("Why did you move into the slums?") and models for people that love of God and neighbor are inseparable.

A TRINITARIAN GOSPEL

> And hope does not disappoint us, because God has poured out his love into our hearts by the Holy Spirit, whom he has given us. You see, at just the right time, when we were still powerless, Christ died for the ungodly (Rom 5:5–6).

In this passage, we see Paul's trinitarian theology: the gift of the Holy Spirit, the love of God the Father, and the suffering of Christ the Son. The apostle models integrated theologizing, since each one leads to the others. We can't lead people into an experience of God's love without the Holy Spirit's enabling. Nor can we lead people to consider suffering for Christ without leading them into the Father's love, which compels us to give ourselves for others. We don't want people to experience the Holy Spirit's power for witness without a compelling vision of doing the works and teachings of Jesus. We want disciples that minister with the power *and* paradigm of Pentecost. Therefore we aim for the Father's love, the Son's suffering, and the Spirit's power as a cohesive whole that testifies to God's shalom.

THE BIBLE STORY[1]

The biblical storyline of a *Nail Scarred Hands Made New* gospel can be described and taught like this:

1. God acts by doing something wonderful and good, like creating the world, calling Israel into being, or sending Christ.
2. This "costly demonstration of unexpected love" reveals his universal project to two parties, though differently and often offensive to one—be it Adam and Eve, Cain and Abel, Jacob and Esau, Jew and gentile, Pharisee and tax collector, the rich man and Lazarus, the prodigal and his brother, the two thieves on the cross, and on and on.
3. This usually creates a crisis between the two, with one receiving God's surprising act and the other rejecting it.
4. God acts to rescue and restore both, in spite of us.
5. We continue to screw up amid many signs of God's inbreaking kingdom.
6. Ultimately, God uses us in all our shortcomings to act wonderfully again to fulfill his promise.

New believers typically receive a handful of principles considered foundational (e.g., read the Bible, pray, congregate in a church, share your faith with others, and, of course, obey God!). I was taught that this should be my foremost concern with new converts.

In contrast to this, we emphasize getting into the biblical story. We want folks to see the overall sweep of biblical history. This is akin to providing a vision of the sea's vastness instead of a boat to cross it.[2] We created a pictorial narrative of the Bible that fits on an 8.5" x 11" sheet of paper. In a concise, visual fashion, this "Bible 101" tool interprets the big story from Genesis to Revelation. In home Bible studies, we pull it out to place a reading within the larger scriptural narrative.

In our teaching, we hold together the narrative of Christ's incarnation, mission, teaching, death, resurrection, and Pentecost. Typical teaching isolates Jesus' death from his ministry and teaching. Story-based images such as "partners at the cliff's edge," "Cornelius' house" and "outside the gate" keep the storyline intact, revealing how the of-

---

1. Newbigin, *Gospel in a Pluralist Society*, 151, 182, 232.
2. Saint-Exupéry, *Citadelle*.

fense of Jesus' ministry led to his death. We don't properly understand the cross apart from understanding Jesus' life and ministry.

When we connect the dots between Jesus' life, teaching, and death, we find our own discipleship journey within the gospel narrative. We recognize our experience of God ("I screwed up, and God had mercy on me.") in Israel's experience ("we screwed up by betraying Christ and God had mercy by restoring us."). We see God's repeated acts of love, from the big event of the cross to his many small and personal acts today.

Discipleship that teaches the biblical story also helps cultivate a community orientation. God's story has room for me as an individual but is always bigger. The church becomes a community that dwells in the biblical story, remembering it and reenacting it through baptism and communion and through congregating to announce the good news.

When the biblical story we teach continues into the second coming of Christ and the glory of that day when all things are made new, the linking of our stories with God's takes on enormously hope-filled meaning—painful and powerful as they may be. The continuity of Jesus' crucified body with his resurrected body enables us to see and affirm the eternal meaning of our cross taken up in Christ's name. Though Jesus' death was unique, we can also affirm that since his short life was not wasted, nor will ours be. Our suffering for the sake of the gospel, even to the point of losing our lives, is redemptive in the sense that it mirrors God's "outside-the-gate" ways and "remains" (1 Cor 13:13) in the realm to which it belongs—the heavenly new creation (Gal 4:26).

The methods used in teaching the above points are critical. When I dictate information that listeners write down, I teach more than the dictated content. I teach a culture of learning. I teach about roles, leadership, power, and more.

We use methods that teach a culture of inquiry and reflection. Resources abound to help Christians become better at teaching so that people learn. Here are a few guidelines we've adopted for the learning environments we create with people:

- We teach a *vision of God*—first and always!
- We teach to the *heart* with story and imagination, aiming at people's deep assumptions about God, relationships, and the world.
- We teach *groups* in order to create community, supplementing this with individual mentoring.

- We teach for *learning*, not simply increased knowledge or information, to encourage thinking and discovering.
- We use mostly *oral* methods, including music; we don't use fill-in-the-blank written materials or the like.
- We create communities around the *functions* of kingdom living (love one another, love your neighbor, etc.), not the *forms* of church life (where attending meetings becomes the sign of faithfulness and commitment).
- We anchor biblical and theological reflection in the *realities* that people live in the slums.

In the end, it's not the might of our ingenuity and cleverness that empowers disciples to live the kingdom or forgive their enemy. We simply want to echo the apostle Paul's parting words to the elders in Ephesus: "After I leave savage wolves will come . . . I am innocent of your blood . . . I have taught the whole counsel of God."

I believe a sure starting point for conveying the whole counsel of God is an incarnated gospel—messengers made flesh, a people inhabiting the Good News for the poor with their hands and feet. I consider this a sure starting point because Christ's birth put into motion what inevitably led to his death and resurrection. When we model Christ's costly humility, we plant the seed in those we disciple of a hope-inspired witness to Christ's nail scarred hands made new.

2012—the InnerCHANGE team in Caracas. L to R; John and Birgit Shorack, Katie McClure, Layyen and Arturo Gutierrez Surga (with little Grecie), Cameron Carter. Noretys Castillo (inset)

Bibliography

Annacondia, Carlos. *Listen to Me, Satan: Exercising Authority over the Devil in Jesus' Name*. Lake Mary, FL: Charisma House, 1998.
Bailey, Kenneth E. *The Cross and the Prodigal: Luke 15 through the Eyes of Middle Eastern Peasants*. Downers Grove, IL: InterVarsity, 2005.
———. *Jesus through Middle Eastern Eyes*. Downers Grove, IL: InterVarsity, 2008.
———. "Four Misconceptions," www.youtube.com/watch?v=HpbJs8tafeg.
Bonino, José Míguez. *Doing Theology in a Revolutionary Situation*. Philadelphia: Fortress, 1975.
Costas, Orlando. *Christ outside the Gate: Mission beyond Christendom*. 1982; repr., Eugene, OR: Wipf & Stock, 2005.
Delgado Linares, Carlos. *Caracas Ayer, Hoy y Siempre*. Caracas, Venezuela: Proyecto Cultural Namar Ediciones, 2001.
Eller, Vernard. *Christian Anarchy: Jesus' Primacy over the Powers*. Grand Rapids: Eerdmans, 1987.
Ellul, Jacques. *The Presence of the Kingdom*. Colorado Springs: Helmers & Howard, 1989.
González, Justo L. *Santa Biblia: The Bible through Hispanic Eyes*. Nashville: Abingdon, 1996.
———. *Mañana: Christian Theology from a Hispanic Perspective*. Nashville: Abingdon, 1990.
———. González, Ondina E. *Christianity in Latin America: A History*. New York: Cambridge University Press, 2008.
Jersak, Brad. *Can You Hear Me? Tuning in to the God Who Speaks*. Grand Rapids: Monarch, 2006.
Kraft, Charles. *Christianity with Power: Your Worldview and Your Experience of the Supernatural*. Ann Arbor: Vine, 1989.
Mangalwadi, Vishal. *Truth and Social Reform*. Minneapolis: Good Books, 1996.
Moreno, Alejandro. *Y salimos a matar: Investigación sobre el delincuente venezolano violento de origen popular*. (vol. 1) Caracas: CIP, 2009.
Newbigin, Lesslie. *The Gospel in a Pluralist Society*. Grand Rapids: Eerdmans, 1989.
Packer, J. I. *Knowing God*. Downers Grove, IL: InterVarsity, 1993.
Pollak-Eltz, Angelina. *La Religiosidad Popular en Venezuela: Un estudio fenomenológico de la religiosidad en Venezuela*. Caracas, Venezuela: San Pablo, 1994.
Saint-Exupéry, Antoine de. *Citadelle*. Paris: Gallimard, 1988.
Stott, John. *The Cross of Christ*. Downers Grove, IL: InterVarsity, 1986.
Van Engen, Charles, and Jude Tiersma. *God So Loves the City: Seeking a Theology for Urban Mission*. 1994; repr., Eugene, OR: Wipf & Stock, 2009.
Van Engen, Charles, Nancy Thomas, and Robert Gallagher. *Footprints of God: A Narrative Theology of Mission*. 1999; repr., Eugene, OR: Wipf & Stock, 2011.

Van Rheenen, Gailyn. *Communicating Christ in Animistic Contexts*. Grand Rapids: Baker, 1991.
Wink, Walter. *The Powers That Be: Theology for a New Millennium*. New York: Random, 1998.
Wright, Tom. *The Challenge of Jesus: Rediscovering Who Jesus Was and Is*. Downers Grove, IL: InterVarsity, 1999.
———. *Following Jesus: Biblical Reflections on Discipleship*. Grand Rapids: Eerdmans, 1994.

www.ingramcontent.com/pod-product-compliance
Lightning Source LLC
Chambersburg PA
CBHW070943160426
43193CB00011B/1790